MAO
TSE-TUNG'S
Cultural Revolution

MAO TSE-TUNG'S

Cultural Revolution

TAI SUNG AN

PEGASUS

A Division of The Bobbs-Merrill Company, Inc., Publishers

To WASHINGTON COLLEGE
and to DANIEL Z. GIBSON
Who Served It So Well
As President for Twenty Years

CONTENTS

PREFACE

THIS BOOK is a brief version of a larger work in progress on Mao Tse-tung's Cultural Revolution, which I plan to complete by the time the Cultural Revolution runs its full course or Chairman Mao passes away from the Chinese scene. The book has but one modest objective: to put the Cultural Revolution in proper perspective, to arrive at *tentative* conclusions about the results of the past five-year course of Mao's so-called "Second Revolution."

The materials which have been used in the preparation of this book fall roughly into the following categories: (a) such primary and original sources in the Chinese language as Chinese Communist newspapers, periodicals, and other publications; (b) Chinese Communist broadcasts; (c) Chinese Communist periodicals, journals, and other publications in English which are regularly published by the Chinese Communists; (d) newspapers, periodicals, journals, books, and others published in Hong Kong both in Chinese and English; (e) Soviet sources both in the Russian language and English; (f) Japanese newspapers, books, journals, and periodicals; (g) various West European (i.e., British, West German, and French) sources; (h) books and articles on Communist China which are published in the United States; and (i) summaries and reports of American newspapers.

x   *Preface*

I would like to acknowledge that in the course of preparing for this book, I have found many news reports on Communist China from Hong Kong-based correspondents of *The New York Times, The Washington Post, The* (Baltimore) *Sun,* and *The Los Angeles Times* helpful. These American China-watchers, particularly Mr. Stanley Karnow, have been doing an excellent job.

Full responsibility for any possible error of fact or interpretation rests, needless to say, with me alone.

It is with sincere gratitude that I wish to acknowledge the generous support and help given to me in my research work on Mao's Cultural Revolution. First of all, a debt of special thanks is due to Washington College, where I am currently teaching, for its financial assistance at critical points in the preparation of the book. I am also grateful to President Emeritus Daniel Z. Gibson and Professor Nathan Smith of Washington College for their sympathetic interest in my research work on Communist China. I should also like to acknowledge my debts for moral support to my wife, Sihn-ja, the late Business Manager Robert C. Simmonds, and Mr. Theodore F. Parker of Washington College. My final note of gratitude goes to Mr. Edward G. McLeroy, editor.

TAI SUNG AN
Chestertown, Maryland

INTRODUCTION

THE GREAT PROLETARIAN CULTURAL REVOLUTION[1] is Communist China's euphemistic description for the recent nationwide purge of Chairman Mao Tse-tung's "revisionist" opponents in the entire Party and government apparatus, which is designed, in the words of Richard D. Baum, "to immunize the [750 million] Chinese people against the pernicious virus of Khrushchev's apostate 'revisionism'."[2] According to the Maoist definition, "revisionism" means hostility to Mao's militant Communist ideology, the aping of Western cultural mores, educational conservatism, friendly feelings toward the Soviet Union, overreliance on technical skills or the use of direct economic incentives in industrial and agricultural managements, and the emphasis on professionalism in military affairs.

On September 6, 1968, *Jen-min Jih-pao* (People's Daily), the official daily newspaper of the Mao Tse-tung regime in Peking, jubilantly declared a decisive nationwide victory (but not final or total victory) in the Cultural Revolution. To re-emphasize the matter, "Marshal"[3] and Defense Minister Lin Piao, Chairman Mao's officially chosen heir, claimed on October 1, 1968 (Peking's National Day), that "our Great Proletarian Cultural Revolution has now scored a great victory."[4]

With the convocation of the Ninth Congress of the Chinese Communist Party in April, 1969, Mao Tse-tung's Cultural Revolution seemed to have largely run its course. The Ninth Party Congress in Peking was widely publicized and hailed by the Maoist Chinese as the triumphal culmination of Mao's tumultuous Cultural Revolution.

In his report delivered on April 1, 1969, at the opening session of the Ninth Party Congress, Lin Piao explained the origin of Mao's Cultural Revolution, described its chaotic "twists and reversals," and then claimed that it had resulted in a "great victory."[5] At the same time, he spelled out a formal end to the most dramatic period of the Cultural Revolution that had convulsed Communist China for the preceding three years. (He implied, however, that the Cultural Revolution would continue in a more orderly fashion.)

The same claims to great victory in Communist China's Cultural Revolution were repeatedly made thereafter.

It is this author's contention that the Maoist claims to great victory in Mao's Cultural Revolution do not survive examination of the evidence, nor does the official prediction of imminent all-round victory. Despite all the propaganda extolling Mao's victory, it is apparent that Chairman Mao has lost his Utopian crusade to remake China in his militant revolutionary image, although he may have won his personal battle against his principal "revisionist" opponent, Liu Shao-ch'i. In recent months, the Maoist leadership has been needlessly noisy about its assertion of great victory in the Cultural Revolution, so much so that one cannot help doubting the truth of the assertion.

NOTES TO INTRODUCTION

1. For a discussion of the term "Great Proletarian Cultural Revolution" see H. C. Chuang, *The Great Proletarian Cultural Revolution: A Terminological Study,* Center for Chinese Studies, Institute of International Studies, University of California, Berkeley, California, August 1967, pp. 1–5.

2. Quoted from Richard D. Baum, "Ideology Redivivus," *Problems of Communism,* May–June 1967, p. 1.

3. All military ranks and badges were abolished in Communist China on June 1, 1965. *New China News Agency,* May 25, 1965.

4. *Peking Review,* October 4, 1968, p. 13.

5. For the full text of Lin Piao's report see *Peking Review,* April 30, 1969, pp. 16–35.

CHAPTER 1

The Historical Background of Mao's Cultural Revolution

THE CURRENT political turmoil in Communist China, or what Peking euphemistically calls the "Great Proletarian Cultural Revolution," is essentially a "spiritual" movement to mold China in Mao Tse-tung's image of total struggle, a perpetual Long March of uncorrupted romantic, militant Communism and, at the same time, Mao's last desperate attempt to restore ideological purity and revolutionary momentum to the sagging Communist movement in China. Chairman Mao's fundamental prescription for the future of Communist China has long been the perpetuation of the revolutionary élan that he believes would offer a "magic" shortcut to the modernization of his country. In recent years, Mao, 77, has been obsessed with the fear that, upon his death, his militant brand of Communism, to which he devoted his entire life, might be repudiated by his colleagues and successors, in the same manner as Stalin was repudiated by Nikita S. Khrushchev, so the Chinese Communist society would drift in the direction of Soviet "bourgeois revisionism." With the possible death of this "revolutionary romanticism," as Robert Jay Lifton aptly puts it, Mao has envisioned "nothing but the total extinction of his own self" and, consequently, suffered from this "survival paranoia."[1] The Cultural Revolution, which began in earnest in the spring of 1966, was

1

launched by Mao in a quest for the rebirth and perpetuation of his Yenan-type militant Communism in China through the elevation of the Maoist doctrine to the status of sacrosanct dogma. During the height of the Cultural Revolution, *Hung Ch'i* (Red Flag), the theoretical journal of the Chinese Communist Party, asserted that "one's attitude toward Mao Tse-tung's Thought should be the yardstick identifying the genuine from the sham revolutionary and the counter-revolutionary, the Marxist-Leninist from the revisionist."[2] Another Maoist publication, *Chieh-fang-chün Pao* (Liberation Army Daily), went one step further than this and said bluntly that every Chinese "must think and act in accordance with the teachings of Mao Tse-tung. If Chairman Mao says it is so, then it is so, and if he says it is not so, then surely it is not so."[3]

Perhaps Chairman Mao Tse-tung brooded over the sad fate of Stalin at the hands of Khrushchev. Branko Bogunovic, a chief editor of *Tangjug*, official news agency of Yugoslavia, who is an able East European China-watcher, is correct in arguing that Mao, in large part, set off the Cultural Revolution primarily in order not to repeat Stalin's "tragedy."[4] According to Mao's judgment, Stalin was "an outstanding Marxist-Leninist fighter," but one of his major "mistakes," mostly committed in the latter part of his life, was failure to understand clearly "the laws of the continuing class struggle in Socialist society" and thus provide a "genuine Marxist-Leninist heir" before he died.[5] This "great tragedy" allowed a "phony" Communist like Khrushchev and his "renegade revisionist clique to effect counter-revolutionary restoration" in the Soviet Union. Mao is now endeavoring to prevent in China a repetition of the Soviet Union's "tragedy," and has chosen an official heir, Defense Minister Lin Piao, who would pursue his dogma of "permanent (or uninterrupted) revolution" without changing its true proletarian colors.

It must be noted that Mao Tse-tung's theory of "permanent revolution" differs from Leon Trotsky's definition of the term, although Nikita S. Khrushchev obliquely compared Maoism to Trotskyism in the fall of 1959, for his anti-Chinese propaganda purpose. The Maoist theory of "permanent revolution," roughly defined, has two important political and philosophical connotations.[6] The first is associated with the pace of domestic revolutionary advance that would take place after the Communists seized power. According to Maoism, there could and would be no "half-way halt" (i.e., the loss of revolutionary momentum and ideological fervor) in the advance toward true Communism, as it is now happening in the Soviet Union. Echoing the rhetoric of Stalin's Great Purge of the 1930s,[7] the Maoist dogma of "permanent revolution" asserts that the "class struggle" will only grow more acute as the building of Communism advances, so the "class enemy" must be destroyed ceaselessly and mercilessly to carry the revolution through to the end.

The second is applied to a Communist revolutionary strategy in the non-Communist world. Communism came to power in China, the world's most populous nation, by Mao Tse-tung's guerrilla warfare ("people's war") tactics of surrounding the cities—the strongholds of the "reactionary or pro-capitalist segment of the national bourgeoisie—from the rural countryside. Now the time has come to apply the Chinese Communist revolutionary experience to the whole world: to encourage and support the Communist-led "people's war" in Asia, Africa, the Middle East, and Latin America ("the rural areas of the world") to encircle and destroy the North American and West European capitalist countries ("the cities of the world").

Mao's theory of "permanent revolution" was so obnoxious to the Soviet Union that the Kremlin leaders, both Khrushchev and his present successors, never acknowledged its validity. Moscow ridiculed Maoism as a "reactionary, irrational, sinocentric petty-bourgeois conception, and an eclectic hodgepodge of Confucianism, anarchism, Trotskyism, petty-bourgeois nationalism, chauvinistic racism, and adventurism."[8] It also said that Communist China under Mao is dominated by aggressive "barracks communism."

Mao Tse-tung's Cultural Revolution was originally bent on nothing less than cleansing the entire Communist Party apparatus—which, he suspected, succumbed to the comfortable "bourgeois" temptations of Soviet-style "revisionism"—and re-forming and revitalizing it with loyal Maoist "revolutionaries." The original aims of the Cultural Revolution also included an ideological revolution for (a) training young Maoist "revolu-tionary successors" and, subsequently, injecting these new young leaders into sweepingly revamped organs of power at all levels; and (b) eliminating all "feudal" and "bourgeois" as well as "revisionist" influences among the Chinese people.[9]

In pursuit of these original objectives, Mao's Cultural Revo-lution purged not only a large number of Mao's closest col-leagues of forty years, but for practical purposes virtually all important provincial, local Party and government officials, who were allegedly "taking the capitalist road." (At the time of the Cultural Revolution, all important Chinese Communist leaders throughout the country held interlocking or concurrent posi-tions in the Party and government.) In so doing, Mao destroyed once and for all the decades-old myth of the monolithic unity of the Chinese Communists behind his leadership.

Quite contrary to *ex post facto* exaggeration and distortion of the Maoist propaganda media, Mao's purged opponents in the Cultural Revolution (anti-Maoists)[10] were not the "bour-geois reactionaries or revisionists who were walking the capital-ist road," but the dedicated Communists and veterans of the legendary Long March of the mid-1930s. Many of them, in fact, used to be anti-Khrushchev "hard-liners" themselves, more Maoists than Chairman Mao himself, in the bitter Sino-Soviet ideological conflict.

In point of fact, the only major "sin" anti-Maoist leaders in the Party and government ever committed, if any, is their "sneaky" disagreement with Mao's radical policies at home and abroad during the period between 1959 and 1965. To put the matter into simple terms, the major policy dispute between Chairman Mao and his "revisionist" opponents prior to the commencement of the Cultural Revolution had been over the issue of revolutionary (dogmatic) radicalism *versus* pragmatic realism.[11]

The Cultural Revolution is not a sudden and inexplicable phenomenon. Its roots can be traced back to the Great Leap Forward and the commune system of 1958.

Communist China's Great Leap Forward and the commune system were a massive economic experiment, purely Maoist in conception. They were designed to mobilize hundreds of millions of Chinese, substituting manpower for capital and technology, and putting politics and ideological incentives in command of agriculture and industry, to modernize the country in a few short years into a first-rate economic power. According to secret Chinese Communist documents containing Mao's speeches, letters, and instructions that have recently become public in the United States, he said at Communist China's Supreme State Conference, January 28, 1958, just before the launching of the Great Leap Forward and the communes:

> Talking about it now, our country is so populous; it has such vast territory and abundant resources, a history of more than 4,000 years, and culture . . . what a boast, though it is not even as good as Belgium. . . . Yet our steel production is so low; . . . so few people are literate. We are inferior when these things are compared, but we have zeal and must catch up with Britain within fifteen years. . . .
>
> Our nation is one with ardor, and there is a fervent tide now. Our nation is like an atom . . . and after the fission of the atomic nucleus of our nation, thermal energy will be released which becomes so formidable that we will be able to do what was beyond our ability before. . . .
>
> There are two methods of leadership; one is a little better than the other. . . . For instance, on the question of cooperativization, some advocated quick action, others slower action. I consider the former better. Strike the iron when it is hot; better to get it done in one stroke than drag on.[12]

Mao's Great Leap Forward and the commune system were a wild Maoist scheme, for they were incapable of sustaining the Chinese economy, let alone making rapid advances. They proved catastrophic failures, due to a great deal of initial unrealistic planning. Along with the natural calamities such as floods and plagues of locusts, they plunged the country into economic disaster, the people came near to starvation, and Communist China lost ten years of industrial growth. Indeed, they were economic mismanagement on a colossal scale, so in December, 1958, Chairman Mao and his adherents began to retreat from them—without, however, openly admitting their failures to this day.

The failure of the Great Leap Forward and the communes shattered the confidence many top Chinese Communist leaders had had in Mao, along with the myth of Maoist infallibility. In 1959, Chairman Mao had serious and active opposition within the Chinese Communist Party. Defense Minister P'eng Teh-huai, a member of the Chinese Communist Party's Politburo, attacked Mao's disastrous Great Leap Forward and commune policies at the Party's Politburo's meeting and Central Committee Plenum held in July and August, 1959, at Lushan, a mountain resort in southern Kiangsi Province.[13] Mao weathered the challenge and purged Defense Minister P'eng and his chief subordinates in September, 1959. After this purge, Lin Piao, a wholehearted public advocate of Maoism, became Defense Minister.[14]

Communist China's principal political leaders who were inwardly opposed to Mao's reckless domestic policies of 1958 nevertheless stood by him in his purge of Defense Minister P'eng. Three explanations seem plausible for this support: (1) Mao Tse-tung still remained a powerful symbol to the 750 million Chinese people as the father of the Chinese People's Republic; (2) most of Mao's radical economic policies of 1958 were already being modified at the time of P'eng's challenge against Mao; and (3) they favored some show of national solidarity in the face of the emerging Sino-Soviet ideological conflict.

But Mao's victory against P'eng was a hollow one. Communist China's party apparatchiks (most of whom have been denounced or purged as pro-Soviet "revisionists walking the capitalist road" during the Cultural Revolution) went along with Mao's frenetic Great Leap Forward and the commune system at their outset, but gradually merged in opposition to him when the ambitious scheme collapsed, even stripping him of much of his authority while loudly glorifying his name. In December, 1958, Mao resigned from his position as Chairman of the Chinese People's Republic, thereby removing himself from practical control of daily state affairs. Liu Shao-ch'i succeeded Mao in this role. The official reason given for Mao's resignation from the government post was that he would henceforth devote himself fully to the study of Communist doctrine. (During the height of the Cultural Revolution, the Maoist press said that Mao was prodded gently out of office. Mao charged in a speech in October, 1966, that his anti-Maoist "revisionist" opponents failed in those years to consult him on important policy questions and treated him as if he were "a dead father at a funeral.")[15] But Mao retained his position as Chairman of the Chinese Communist Party. He soon faced a hostile majority within the Party apparatus, losing control of the organization he had dominated since the mid-1930s. In short, he did in fact suffer a drastic loss of personal power in December, 1958. But he refused to concede defeat and, therefore, made a strategic retreat to regroup his forces and thus reassert his claim to ideological infallibility, biding his time.

To make matters worse, the fiasco of the Great Leap Forward and the commune system was followed by a series of foreign policy setbacks in the first half of the 1960s, which were caused by Mao's aggressive "adventurism" in world affairs. These setbacks included deterioration of Sino-Soviet relations, the bloody fiasco of the coup by the pro-Chinese Indonesian Communist Party, expulsion of Chinese Communist diplomats from several African countries on the charge of subversive

activities, and the desertion of Peking's three formerly close
allies in the Sino-Soviet conflict: North Korea, North Vietnam,
and the Japanese Communist Party.[16]

Following these Maoist setbacks at home and abroad,
Peking's apparatchiks (Mao's erstwhile close comrades and followers) led by Liu Shao-ch'i and Teng Hsiao-p'ing came to
realize that Maoism was obsolete as a guide to action for Communist China as it progressed toward modernization and that
their country was heading toward catastrophe if it followed
Mao's radical policy line. Liu Shao-ch'i, Mao's former heir
apparent, who became the chief target of the Cultural Revolution as "the top Party leader in authority who is taking the
capitalist road" and as "China's Khrushchev,"[17] stated:

> Responsible leaders should combine revolutionary fervor
> with pragmatism. One should avoid empty slogans and big
> talk, and should not launch projects lightheartedly if one is
> not sure of their attainment.[18]

During the months of 1960, the Chinese economy plunged
deeper and deeper into chaos. The withdrawal of Soviet aid
and three years of natural calamities had made any reconstruction of a stable economy out of the shambles of the Great Leap
Forward and the commune system an almost insurmountable
task. Anti-Maoist Party leaders desperately searched for adequate measures to bolster the economy. Consequently, they
advocated a more pragmatic, moderate, and rational approach
for the solution of Communist China's problems of modernization, stressing the importance of an incentive system based on
wage and status differentials, technical expertise, and scientific
skills in order to achieve economic progress. The Secretary-
General of the Chinese Communist Party, Teng Hsiao-p'ing,
reportedly said in the early 1960s: "Private farming is all right,
so long as it raises output, just as it does not matter whether the
cat is black or white, so long as it catches mice."[19]

During the period 1959–66, in fact, Communist China's anti-
Maoist political leaders had kept practical matters of policy in

their own hands and gradually taken steps to modify Mao's radical domestic policy line to repair the economic disaster caused by the Great Leap Forward and the communes, while still paying lip service to Maoism and the personality cult of Mao and also attacking Soviet "revisionism" as bitterly as Mao himself, at least for the record. (To these anti-Maoist leaders, the Mao cult simply meant to be a minor concession to Mao in indulging his appetite for personal deification, thereby keeping him, and, moreover, the Chinese population, in line. Ironically, it was precisely this demigod cult that Mao used as a major weapon for his reconquest of power in later years.) Under their relatively liberal and rational program, which permitted the restitution of private gardens to peasants, the operation of limited free markets, and the increase of other incentives to boost production, Communist China was able to achieve a moderate economic recovery by the time Mao started the Cultural Revolution.

At the same time, relaxation of controls over intellectuals in the fields of art and literature followed. In the early 1960s the anti-Maoist intellectuals, especially well-known Chinese Communist historians and writers in Peking, obliquely ridiculed and attacked Mao's wild Great Leap Forward and the communes in their publications of allegorical plays, using the traditional Chinese method of *ying-she* (historical analogy).[20] What was more significant, during the same period an elderly Chinese Communist philosopher at the Higher Party School, Yang Hsien-chen, expounded the "harmony of opposites" or "two-merge-into-one" thesis (the doctrine of "compromise-ism"), in direct opposition to the Maoist doctrine of "one-divides-into-two" which stressed the need for constant struggle between the contending aspects of contradictions—particularly those of an "antagonistic" nature.[21]

Furthermore, America's escalation of the Vietnam war in early 1965 and the fear of possible war with the United States over Vietnam reportedly led anti-Maoist Party and military leaders to advocate a Sino-Soviet rapprochement for a resumption of Soviet aid and protection and a united Communist front on the Vietnam war.[22] What was equally important, top and high-ranking military officers, e.g., Chief of the General Staff Lo Jui-ch'ing, were laughing at Mao Tse-tung's military doctrine based on his long experience of guerrilla warfare—which, among other things, maintained that manpower, politics, and ideological indoctrination rather than machines, weapons, and military technique were what decided victory or defeat in war.[23] These military officers insisted on the strategic importance of nuclear weapons in modern warfare and considered the Maoist military doctrine of "people's war" dangerously anachronistic as the defense strategy for Communist China in the nuclear age.[24]

From the standpoint of Mao Tse-tung and his loyal dogmatic supporters, however, the development in Communist China during the period of 1959–65 showed an alarming trend toward the kind of "bourgeois revisionism" now prevailing in the Soviet Union and Eastern Europe. They attacked the system of material incentives as comparable to "rat poison" and reaffirmed that "revolution must command production," denouncing creeping "tendencies towards capitalism" reflected in private plots for peasants, free markets, and other incentives to industrial enterprise. In short, Mao saw Communist China's new liberal trend as undermining the country's ideological commitment to his dogma of "permanent revolution" and thus leading mainland China down the path of Khrushchev-type "revisionism."

In the first half of the 1960s, Mao and his loyal supporters also clung to the dogmatic and militant "world view" and refused to soften Communist China's aggressive anti-imperialist and anti-revisionist stands. To Chairman Mao, a truce or compromise with the Soviet Union was unthinkable and unpardonable, partly because it was tantamount to an ideological sellout and partly because he argued that there would and could be no compromise between "truth" (Communist China) and "error" (the Soviet Union), unless the Kremlin surrendered.

A romantic revolutionary, Mao Tse-tung believes in the superiority of politics, ideology, and manpower over technology, specialization, machines, and weapons.[25] Since the establishment of the People's Republic of China in 1949, Chairman Mao has sought to build a "true" Communist state based on egalitarianism, proclaiming that his ideas are the panacea for the solution of virtually all the problems of Chinese society. He has long contended that spiritual force and ideological incentives can transform human nature, so his brand of revolutionary fundamentalism can inspire and induce Communist China's 750 million to perform all sorts of miracles. The central tenet of Maoism is that "the force of the spirit can be transformed into tremendous material strength," or that, as Stuart R. Schram succinctly puts, "the subjective can create the objective."[26] (Mao Tse-tung's wild Great Leap Forward and the communes were conceived on the basis of this tenet. Later, the Maoist press and Mao's ardent supporters absolved Mao and Maoism from any responsibility for the failure of the Great Leap Forward and the commune system by attributing the failure to sabotage by "class enemies," "incorrect" implementation of the plans by the lower Party cadres, three years of natural calamities, and the sudden complete withdrawal of Soviet economic aid and advisers.) One of the Maoist myths stemming from this notion of "voluntarism" is that Mao's guerrilla warfare strategy overcame many insurmountable obstacles and achieved a final victory against the far superior Chinese Nationalists by placing reliance upon the "human or subjective factors"—i.e., brilliant and "correct" leadership, conscious and dedicated activism, moral rectitude and austerity, and *espirit de corps.*

The Thought of Mao Tse-tung is based essentially on the experience of the long guerrilla war first against the Chinese Nationalists, then against the Japanese invasion, and then once more against the Kuomintang in the final civil war. During the Yenan era of bitter struggle for Communist power, Chairman Mao observed that the key to survival as well as victory lay in such spiritual qualities as indomitable human will, personal dedication, self-sacrifice, and austerity, rather than in such materialistic factors as professional expertise and sophisticated weapons.

To Mao Tse-tung, his notion of guerrilla warfare is not solely a military strategy but a broader conceptual frame of reference for political, economic, and social mobilization. "Just as he regarded Yenan as China in microcosm while he was there," as Stanley Karnow, the *Washington Post's* able China and Southeast Asia correspondent, cogently observes, "so Mao later came to consider China to be Yenan in macrocosm" as he sought to apply the basic features of guerrilla warfare to industry and agriculture on a national scale. Armed with superior political morale, will, and revolutionary consciousness, Mao insists, the 750 million Chinese people can and will perform economic, military, or any miracles, overcoming all technical and physical limits.[27]

Mao Tse-tung, who led the Chinese Communist revolution to ultimate victory,[28] has a limitless ego and tends to have the vision of immortal transcendance in his revolutionary doctrine, whereas his "revisionist" opponents wanted to put Maoism in proper historical perspective and thus deny it as a doctrine of universal truth. (It is therefore no wonder that the Cultural Revolution has been accompanied by an unparalleled publicity campaign to immortalize Mao and his ideology.)[29] Because of his arrogant assumption to all-time infallibility of his dogma, Mao takes any opposition to his romantic revolutionary fundamentalism as the virtual equivalent of treason to the state. Furthermore, he contends that Soviet-style "revisionism" is a dangerous and poisonous evil—and that Communist China will return to capitalism unless it suppresses and eradicates this evil.

In the early 1960s Mao felt a deep sense of betrayal by the whole Chinese Communist Party machine which slipped out of his control and, from then onward, began to distrust all his former closest associates within the Party as "wolves in sheep's clothing" and "tigers with smiling faces," surreptitiously seducing the unsuspecting Chinese masses with their "sugar-coated bullets" of Khrushchev-brand "revisionism."[30] At the same time, he realized that, unless drastic measures were taken immediately or in the near future to remove these anti-Maoist "renegades," they could be his successors ready to initiate "de-Maoization" thoroughly. He felt he had to act to regain control of the Chinese Communist movement to insure the continuation of his ideals after his death. To this end, he needed a power base outside the Party apparatus, and for this he relied on his demigod image among the Chinese people and also turned to the Chinese People's Liberation Army which, under the leadership of the new Defense Minister Lin Piao, stood alone in the early 1960s as the foremost Maoist revolutionary organization in China. (It is to be noted that Mao has consistently stressed for the past forty-odd years that "political power grows out of the barrel of the gun.")[31]

One of Mao's most trusted lieutenants, Lin Piao, who took over the army in 1959, indoctrinated it with a program for "creative study and application of Mao Tse-tung's Thought." It was under Lin Piao's leadership that the Chinese People's Liberation Army recovered quickly from the effects of both the Great Leap Forward and the communes of 1958 and the subsequent purge of Defense Minister P'eng Teh-huai and his chief subordinates. What was more important, the army under his leadership became the model Maoist organization, and beginning in December, 1963, was made a model of ideological correctness and revolutionary gallantry for the whole nation (including the ruling Communist Party) to emulate. In the army, Lin Piao attempted with considerable success to restore popular confidence in Mao's leadership after the collapse of the Great Leap Forward and the commune system by refining and expanding the cult of Mao, while Communist China's supreme leader, still Party Chairman, stayed strategically in the background. As opposition to Chairman Mao grew stronger within the Party establishment and his distrust of the Party bureaucracy as revolutionary vanguard grew, he established a closer relationship with the new Defense Minister and his army to silence anti-Maoist opposition within the Party.

As the army was becoming an obedient weapon to wield against his "revisionist" opponents within the Party, Chairman Mao devised a strategy based on the combination of caution, persistence, ambiguity, and deception that, in the words of Michel Oksenberg, "would unfold slowly, so that he could not confront a united opposition and could eliminate his enemies one by one."[32] In other words, this strategy faithfully followed his famous guerrilla warfare precepts. He alternately attacked and withdrew, abandoned and retrenched, striving with each push to gain a bit more ground against his adversaries.

As soon as the economic situation took a turn for the better in the early 1960s, Mao began to strive to stem the permissive tide prevailing in the country at the time by renewing his campaigns to revolutionize culture, reindoctrinate intellectuals, and halt the "spontaneous tendencies toward capitalism" among the industrial workers and peasants. In the Tenth Plenary Session of the Eighth Central Committee of the Chinese Communist Party held in September, 1962, Mao reiterated his warning, "Never forget class struggle." This was followed by a rectification campaign of unorthodox tendencies which had risen in the art and literary fields and the Socialist Education Movement set in motion throughout China in the winter of 1963–64. Aimed at cleansing all Chinese of any anti-Maoist tendencies, the Movement called upon them to "arm themselves with Mao Tse-tung's Thought."

Mao began to exhibit a harder line toward his "revisionist" opponents within the Party.by launching a mass campaign to "learn from the People's Liberation Army" in February, 1964.[33] The "Learn from the PLA" Campaign was designed to extol the Maoist revolutionary virtues which Lin Piao's army embodied and which Mao wanted to extend to the whole nation for emulation. This campaign was soon followed by concrete steps to establish a new political apparatus in governmental, economic, communication, and educational organs modeled directly on the army's political organization and staffed primarily by its officers.

In the summer of 1964 Mao also launched a campaign to "cultivate revolutionary successors."[34] In the early 1960s Mao worried that the new generation of Chinese, almost all of whom joined the revolution after the final victory of the Chinese Communists against the Nationalists in 1949, would relax their vigilance against "class enemies" at home and abroad after his death. Accordingly, this campaign was intended to instill in this younger generation the same revolutionary spirit of the Yenan era for the avowed purpose of training millions of "legitimate" successors, capable of carrying on the cause of Mao's militant Communism.

Apparently, these rectification and indoctrination campaigns did not produce the expected results of reinvigorating the revolutionary spirit of the Chinese masses, apparently because Mao's close associates in the Party subtly but solidly resisted and sabotaged Mao's battle calls through delay, deceit, and so on. In 1963, it is now revealed, Mao complained that "very little had been achieved so far in socialist transformation of the country. . . . Was not it absurd that many Communists showed enthusiasm in advancing feudal and capitalist arts, but no zeal in promoting socialist art?"[35] Speaking to Edgar Snow in January, 1965, Mao Tse-tung candidly worried that Communist China's younger generation might lack the necessary "revolutionary fervor" to continue his brand of militant Communism.[36] By 1965, in short, Mao realized that the Chinese Communist Party was completely out of his control and also suspected that his entire Communist Party apparatus succumbed to the manifold temptations of "revisionism," after having slain the monster of capitalism, and avidly waiting for his death so they could initiate "de-Maoization" and adopt Khrushchev-type "revisionism."

Mao's fear that the entrenched Party bureaucracy was subverting his "permanent revolution" and guiding the country toward capitalism was openly spelled out for the first time on July 14, 1964, in a long article entitled "On Khrushchev's Phony Communism and Its Historical Lessons for the World."[37] Though ostensibly an attack on Nikita S. Khrushchev and his "revisionism," it also represented an oblique assault against Liu Shao-ch'i, Teng Hsiao-p'ing, and their "revisionist" colleagues in the upper echelons of the Chinese Communist Party who, Mao believed, were the real enemies of Maoism. Proof of the double-edged nature of the anti-revisionist stand in this long article was provided by the following one key passage:

> Is our [Chinese] society today thoroughly clean [from Khrushchev-type revisionism]? No, it is not. Classes and class struggle still remain, the activities of the overthrown reactionary classes plotting a comeback still continue, and we still have speculative activities by old and new bourgeois elements and desperate forays by embezzlers, grafters and degenerates. There are also cases of degeneration in a few primary organizations; what is more, these degenerates do their utmost to find protectors and agents in the higher leading [Party and government] bodies [of the nation]. We should not in the least slacken our vigilance against such phenomena but must keep fully alert. *At the same time, it must be declared with utmost urgency that our Communist Party will be in great need of purification; otherwise, the revolutionary achievements won through long hard struggle under the leadership of our beloved Chairman Mao Tse-tung will be in danger of being lost.*[38]

Viewed in historical perspective, this long article signaled the coming Cultural Revolution in the above one key passage.

In 1965 Mao was quietly awaiting the opportunity to launch his Cultural Revolution in order to purge the "reactionary" majority within the ruling Chinese Communist Party apparatus and to uproot the influence of "revisionism" in his country.

The key policy debate over the Vietnam crisis and other domestic issues took place at a secret meeting of the Central Committee of the Chinese Communist Party in September,

1965. At this crucial meeting, Mao Tse-tung was in the minority, and the majority sided with his "revisionist" opponents headed by Liu Shao-ch'i.[39]

It was at this frustrating and angry moment that Chairman Mao had decided that the time had finally come to begin his comprehensive, violent purge of the entire Party apparatus with the help of Defense Minister Lin Piao and his army. Out of Mao's alliance with Lin Piao's army in the spring of 1966 came the Great Proletarian Cultural Revolution (or Mao's "Second Revolution")—the grand design to save China, now and for all time, from the danger of "revisionism" with a new wave of terror and turmoil. It was the Chinese People's Liberation Army that first issued the little red book of *Quotations from Chairman Mao Tse-tung* which became the bible of the Cultural Revolution, and in the first critical stage of Mao's "Second Revolution" the army newspaper *Chieh-fang-chün Pao* joined (and temporarily supplanted) the Party newspaper and journal, *Jen-min Jih-pao* and *Hung Ch'i*, as an official Maoist national organ.

On the eve of the Cultural Revolution, by and large, Mao Tse-tung represented the "opposition" minority that stood up and "rebelled" against the "revisionist" majority in the Party establishment. That is to say, Mao acted as a courageous David who dared challenge the terrible Goliath—the all-powerful Chinese Communist Party. When the "rebellion" began, Mao used Lin Piao's army as the sling.

When the Cultural Revolution was in full swing, one of the Maoist organs declared:

> Lu Houn [the early Chinese Communist literary figure] never appeased the enemy and never let him get away with anything. He felt not the slightest remorse when an enemy was badly battered, nor did he even stop the fighting because the enemy seemed to be at his last breath. He believed in "beating the wild dog even though it is already in the water," and "once you start beating it, beat it to the

death." In our Great Proletarian Cultural Revolution, we should develop this spirit of Lu Hsun of "beating the wild dog in the water to death" and never show softness or mercy to the enemy.[40]

NOTES TO CHAPTER 1

1. Robert Jay Lifton, *Revolutionary Immortality* (New York: Vintage Books, 1968), pp. 20, 94.

2. *Hung Ch'i*, July 1, 1966.

3. *Chieh-fang-chün Pao*, September 20, 1966.

4. Branko Bogunovic, "China Assessed: More Revolution with Mao on Top," *The Washington Post*, September 3, 1967, p. 12 (Sunday Outlook Section). Mr. Bogunovic was a Yugoslav correspondent in Peking from 1957 to 1960 and again from 1963 to the spring of 1967 when the Chinese Communists refused to renew his residence permit apparently because he "knew too much."

5. *Hung Ch'i*, May 18, 1967; and *Jen-min Jih-pao*, June 4, 1967.

6. For the Maoist theory of "permanent revolution," see Hsu Li-chun, "Is it Correct to Speak of 'Having Already Reached Communism'?" *Hung Ch'i*, No. 12, 1958, pp. 20–24; *Peking Review*, June 3, 1958, pp. 14–15; *Hsueh-hsi*, October 10, 1958; *Jen-min Jih-pao*, September 28, 1959; and June 12, 1969; "United under Lenin's Revolutionary Banner," in *Long Live Leninism* (Peking: Foreign Languages Press, 1960), pp. 94–95; *Ten Glorious Years, 1949–59* (Peking: Foreign Languages Press, 1960), pp. 4, 271–282, 296; Mao Tse-tung, *Selected Works* (New York: International Publishers, 1956), Vol. V, p. 364; Mao Tse-tung, *On the Correct Handling of Contradictions Among the People* (Peking: Foreign Languages Press, 1964), pp. 22, 37; Lin Piao, "Long Live the Victory of the People's War!" *Hung Ch'i* and *Jen-min Jih-pao*, September 3, 1965; Mao Tse-tung's speech at Supreme State Conference of January 28, 1958, reprinted in *Chinese Law and Government, Winter* 1968–69, pp. 13–14; and *Quotations from Chairman Mao Tse-tung* (Peking: Foreign Languages Press, 1966), pp. 16–17.

7. Joseph Stalin, *Problems of·Leninism* (11th Edition; Moscow: Foreign Languages Publishing House, 1953), pp. 317, 797; Joseph Stalin, *Works* (Moscow: Foreign Languages Publishing House, 1955), Vol. XII, p. 381; and *Short History of the Communist Party of the Soviet Union* (Moscow: Foreign Languages Publishing House, 1943), p. 311.

8. See, for example, *Pravda*, September 8, 1966, in the *Current Digest of the Soviet Press* (hereafter cited as the *CDSP*), October 12, 1966, pp. 3–5; *Pravda*, January 28, 1967, in the *CDSP*, February 15, 1967, p. 8; *Pravda*, February 16, 1967, in the *CDSP*, March 8, 1967, pp. 6–9;

Pravda, June 25, 1967, in the *CDSP,* July 19, 1967, pp. 3–6; *Pravda,* August 6, 1967, in the *CDSP,* September 13, 1967, pp. 3–5; *Izvestia,* July 4, 1967, in the *CDSP,* July 26, 1967, pp. 7–9; *Kommunist,* April 1968, in the *CDSP,* May 29, 1968, pp. 3–7; May 1968, in the *CDSP,* June 26, 1968, pp. 9–13; January 1969, in the *CDSP,* March 12, 1969, pp. 10–15; May 1969, in the *CDSP,* June 18, 1969, pp. 3–7; *Izvestia,* May 23, 1968, in the *CDSP,* June 12, 1968, pp. 5–7; and *Pravda,* January 11, 1969, in the *CDSP,* January 29, 1969, pp. 3–6.

9. See, for example, the August 8, 1966, "Decision of the Central Committee of the Chinese Communist Party Concerning the Great Proletarian Cultural Revolution," reprinted in *Peking Review,* August 12, 1966, pp. 6–11.

10. It must be stressed that Mao Tse-tung's purged opponents in the Cultural Revolution never declared themselves anti-Maoists publicly or at closed party meetings. The term "anti-Maoist" in this book is used arbitrarily by this author simply to denote Chinese Communist leaders who disagreed with Chairman Mao's radical policies.

11. See Benjamin I. Schwartz, "China and West in the Thought of Mao Tse-tung," in Ping-ti Ho and Tang Tsou (ed.), *China in Crisis* (Chicago: University of Chicago Press, 1968), Vol. 1, Book 1, pp. 365–379; G. K. Yang, "Cultural Revolution and Revisionism," *ibid.,* Vol. 1, Book 2, pp. 501–524; and A. Doak Barnett, *China After Mao* (Princeton: Princeton University Press, 1967), pp. 3–287.

12. Cited in *Chinese Law and Government,* Vol. 1, No. 4, Winter 1968–69, pp. 11, 13.

13. For the details see *Kung-tso T'ung-hsun* (Military Correspondence), Peking, No. 3, January 7, 1961, p. 3; and No. 24, June 18, 1961, p. 1; David A. Charles, "The Dismissal of Marshal P'eng Teh-huai," *The China Quarterly,* No. 8 (October–December 1961), pp. 63–76; and J. D. Simmonds, "P'eng Teh-huai: A Chronological Re-Examination," *ibid.,* No. 37 (January–March 1969), pp. 120–138.

14. For a study of the rapid rise of Lin Piao see Ralph L. Powell, "The Increasing Power of Lin Piao and the Party Soldiers," *The China Quarterly,* No. 34 (April–June, 1968), pp. 38–65; and Martin Ebon, *Lin Piao: The Life and Writings of China's New Ruler* (New York: Stein and Day, 1970), pp. 1–378.

15. *Current Background,* American Consulate General, Hong Kong, No. 891, October 8, 1969, p. 71; and *The New York Times,* January 6, 1967, pp. 1–2.

16. See this author's article, "New Winds in Pyongyang?" *Problems of Communism,* July–August 1966, pp. 68–71; William E. Griffith, "Sino-Soviet Relations, 1964–1965," *The China Quarterly,* January–March 1966, pp. 66–76; Kyosuke Hirotsu, "Japan," *Survey,* January 1965, pp. 123–130; Arthur J. Dommen, "Japan's Communists: Rich and Cautious," *Reporter,* April 6, 1967, pp. 33–37; Omori Minoru, "Mao's Worst Crisis," *The New Republic,* January 28, 1967, pp. 17–19; and J. A. Stockwen,

"The Communist Party of Japan," *Problems of Communism,* January–February 1967, pp. 1–11.

17. The Twelfth Plenary Session of the Eighth Central Committee of the Chinese Communist Party, which was held from October 13 to October 31, 1968, formally expelled Liu Shao-ch'i from the Party and from all Party and state posts, including his position as the formal head of the Chinese People's Republic. The Committee denounced him by name as a "traitor, renegade and scab," and a "lackey of imperialism, modern revisionism and the Kuomintang"—Chiang Kai-shek's Chinese Nationalist Party. *Hung Ch'i,* October 14, 1968; and *Peking Review,* November 1, 1968, supplement, pp. v-viii.

18. Quoted in *Studies on Chinese Communism,* March 1, 1967, published by the Institute for the Study of Chinese Communist Problems, Taipei, Taiwan.

19. *Jen-min Jih-pao, Hung Ch'i,* and *Chieh-fang-chün Pao,* November 23, 1967.

20. See Yao Wen-yuan, "Criticism of the New Historical Play 'The Dismissal of Hai Jui'," *Shangahai Wen Hui Pao,* November 10, 1965; Chün-tu Hsüeh, "The Cultural Revolution and Leadership Crisis in Communist China," *Political Science Quarterly,* June 1967, pp. 173–177; Stephen Uhalley, "The Cultural Revolution and the Attack on the 'Three Family Village'," *The China Quarterly,* June–September, 1966, pp. 149–161; and Merle Goldman, "The Fall of Chou Yang," *The China Quarterly,* June–September, 1966, pp. 132–148.

21. See Donald J. Munro, "The Yang Hsien-chen Affair," *The China Quarterly,* April–June 1965, pp. 75–82.

22. See, for example, Lo Jui-ch'ing, "Commemorate the Victory over German Fascism! Carry the Struggle against U.S. Imperialism through to the End," *Peking Review,* May 14, 1965, pp. 7–15; Lo Jui-ch'ing, "China Stands Ready to Smash U.S. War Schemes," *Peking Review,* August 6, 1965, p. 5; Lo Jui-ch'ing, "The People Defeated Japanese Fascism and They Can Certainly Defeat U.S. Imperialism Too," *Peking Review,* September 3, 1965, pp. 38–39; and *Jen-min Jih-pao,* April 19, 1967. See also Tang Tsou (ed.), *China in Crisis,* II, (Chicago: University of Chicago Press, 1968), pp. 23–72, 237–268; and Donald S. Zagoria, *Vietnam Triangle* (New York: Pegasus, 1967), pp. 63–98.

23. See *Chieh-fang-chün Pao,* August 1, 1966; *Peking Review,* August 5, 1966, pp. 1–10; and *Jen-min Jih-pao,* August 1, 1967, and November 3, 1967. See also this writer's article entitled "Chairman Mao Purges Military Professionalism," *Military Review,* August 1968, pp. 88–98.

24. *Ibid.*

25. See Stuart R. Schram, *The Political Thought of Mao Tse-tung* (New York: Praeger, 1960), pp. 1–330; Rene Goldman, "Mao, Maoism and Mao-ology; A Review Article," *Pacific Affairs,* Winter 1968–69, pp. 560–574; and "What Is Maoism? A Symposium," *Problems of Communism,* September–October 1966, pp. 1–30.

26. Schram, *op. cit.*, p. 80.

27. See, for example, Meng Kuei and Hsiao Lin, "On Sun Yeh-fang's Reactionary Political Stand and Economic Programs," *Peking Review,* October 21, 1966, pp. 21–25; and October 28, 1966, pp. 32–35.

28. For Mao's personal and political biography see Stuart Schram, *Mao Tse-tung* (New York: Simon and Schuster, 1966), pp. 1–326.

29. On December 25, 1967, for example, Peking reported that in 1967 alone Communist China had published 86,400,000 sets of the Selected Works of Mao Tse-tung—more than seven times the number published in the whole of the fifteen years before the Cultural Revolution started. In addition, Communist China had published 350 million copies of the little red book of Quotations from Chairman Mao Tse-tung. These works had been published in Chinese, Chinese minority languages, and foreign languages and distributed in China and "in 148 countries and regions throughout the world." *New China News Agency,* December 25, 1967.

30. *Chieh-fang-chün Pao,* June 7, 1966.

31. Mao Tse-tung, *Selected Works* (New York: International Publishers, 1954), Vol. I, p. 75.

32. Quoted from Michel Oksenberg, *China,* Headline Series No. 203, Foreign Policy Association, New York City, December 1970, p. 38.

33. *Jen-min Jih-pao,* February 1, 1964; and John Gittings, "The 'Learn from the Army' Campaign," *The China Quarterly,* April–June 1964, pp. 153–159.

34. *Jen-min Jih-pao,* May 20, 1964.

35. *Chieh-fang-chün Pao,* June 6, 1966; and *Peking Review,* August 22, 1966, p. 36.

36. Edgar Snow, "Interview with Mao," *The New Republic,* February 27, 1965, p. 23.

37. *Hung Ch'i* and *Jen min Jih pao,* July 11, 1961.

38. (Emphasis added.) *Ibid.*

39. Chiang Ching, the wife of Mao Tse-tung, indirectly admitted that the Maoists did not command a majority at a secret meeting of the Central Committee of the Chinese Communist Party in September 1965. In her speech of November 28, 1966, she made the plea for all forces to rally behind her husband's Cultural Revolution and added that in referring to the question of majority and minority one could not discuss this independently of class viewpoint. She noted: "It is necessary to see who has grasped the truth of Marxism-Leninism and Mao Tse-tung's thought, who is genuinely carrying out the correct line of Chairman Mao." See *Peking Radio,* December 4, 1966; and *Peking Review,* December 9, 1969, pp. 6, 9. The Decision of the Central Committee of the Chinese Communist Party Concerning the Great Proletarian Cultural Revolution of August 8, 1966 stated: "The minority should be defended, because sometimes truth belongs to them." *Jen-min Jih-pao,* August 9, 1956, and *Peking Review,* August 12, 1966, p. 8.

40. *Jen-min Jih-pao,* October 19, 1966.

CHAPTER 2

The Red Guard Stage of
the Cultural Revolution

In undertaking the Cultural Revolution—the most extensive political purge in the twenty-two-year history of the Chinese Communist regime and more or less comparable to the Stalinist purge of the 1930s, Mao had used extra-Party force (the "masses") to purge his own Party machine (the establishment), because the Party apparatus could not be trusted to purge itself. (He had also relied on his overwhelming prestige and the force of his will.) In the summer and fall of 1966, Mao hastily organized and mobilized the Red Guards (by closing down China's educational system) and other pro-Mao mass organizations in order to destroy his "revisionist" opponents within the entire Party apparatus and to obliterate every other alleged "bourgeois" vestige. (The Chinese People's Liberation Army still remained on the sidelines.) The Red Guards were composed mostly of teen-age high-school boys and girls, and other pro-Mao mass "revolutionary rebel" organizations were run and staffed largely by non-Party people, ordinary citizens, factory workers, demobilized soldiers, and other functional groups. Mao urged them to "put destruction first, and in the process you have construction."[1] To rationalize the "rebellion" of these pro-Mao elements against the old Communist Party establishment, Mao's statement made at Yenan on Stalin's sixtieth birthday was widely quoted: "In the last analysis, all the truths of Marxism-Leninism can be summed up in one sentence: To rebel is justified."[2]

The excitable Red Guards took very seriously their designation as the "revolutionary successors" (or the "inheritors of the revolution"), who would not succumb to the "sugar-coated bullets" of enemies at home and abroad, and promised Mao that "they would carry the Cultural Revolution through to the end and would be the Red successors to take over the torch of revolution." They rampaged about the country, attacking Party and government apparatus at all levels, "dragging out" anti-Mao "monsters and freaks" for denunciation as "revisionists" or "capitalist power-holders," staging massive demonstrations in support of Mao and his radical Cultural Revolution, and breaking into schools, museums, libraries, and private homes to destroy antiques, religious articles such as ancestral tablets and books by "reactionary" or "bourgeois" authors.

Unlike the Stalinist purge in the 1930s, Mao's purge faced unexpectedly strong and varied opposition from the old ruling Party and government bureaucracy and from much of the population. Mao's intended victims, many of whom had been in office for some seventeen or eighteen years, refused to submit meekly to the Maoist purge, and fought back, using the political and economic power that remained to them, in a way that was never possible for the victims of Stalin's Great Purge. By December, 1966, the anti-Maoist opposition throughout the country had resisted the Maoist assault and had organized a huge campaign to protect themselves from the purge by gaining active or tacit support from workers and peasants, while the Red Guards and other pro-Mao mass "revolutionary rebel" groups bombarded provincial and local Party and government authorities.[3]

Among several weapons used by anti-Maoist provincial and local leaders was one that the Maoist press denounced as the tactic of "economism"—that is, inciting factory, railway, and dock workers to stoppage, absenteeism, strikes, sabotage of production, and even to bank robbery; and arbitrarily increasing factory workers' wages and promoting apprentices to full pay to enlist their support and protect themselves against the invading Red Guard "little revolutionary generals."[4] Obviously, this tactic of "economism" was used by the anti-Maoists to disrupt the nation's economy, to lead the Chinese masses astray from "the main orientation" of the pro-Mao leftist "rebellion," and to undermine Mao's Cultural Revolution.

Another tactic used by the anti-Mao opposition was to induce or permit educated youths and other urban elements, who had been sent to the countryside for farm and construction work, to return to the cities, thereby swamping transportation and distribution systems and encouraging general social dislocation.[5]

In the rural areas, anti-Maoists enlisted peasant support by distributing state funds and surplus grains. This practice, also denounced as "economism" by the Maoist press, damaged the rural economy in many provinces. In many rural areas, the farmers, undoubtedly encouraged by anti-Mao Party-government leaders, stormed the commune storehouses to seize and divide up both the seed grain and the grain reserves, distributed the commune land among themselves for their own private agricultural production, and established open black markets.[6]

Units of pro-Mao Red Guards in some provinces were attacked by workers and peasants. By drawing on a resentment of "outsiders" or "carpetbaggers" felt by wider circles of the local populace, anti-Maoist provincial and local Party leaders in some areas organized their own "Red Guards" and "Red Workers' Militias" to attack, beat up, and jail Mao Tse-tung's militant Red Guards coming in from outside.[7]

A subtler and shrewder anti-Maoist tactic was for provincial and local Party leaders to acquiesce in, or pretend to welcome, the takeover by Mao's Red Guard units and other pro-Mao mass "rebel" groups and then to stage-manage a "fake seizure of power."[8]

In short, the anti-Maoist counterattack was surprisingly re-sourceful, formidable, and tenacious; it virtually stalled Mao's Cultural Revolution for several months. By the end of 1966, Chairman Mao found that the old ruling Party apparatus he planned to demolish was far more deeply rooted than he had anticipated. (The Maoists called this period the "Black Wind of December.")

Chairman Mao retaliated in December, 1966, by rescinding his former prohibition on "revolutionary" (Red Guard) inter-ference in industry and agriculture, and ordered the Red Guards and other pro-Mao leftists to bring the Cultural Revo-lution into factories, mines, collective farms, and communes— the bailiwicks of anti-Mao provincial and local Party leaders —to crack anti-Maoist Party strength among workers and peas-ants and to seize power for themselves.[9]

The attempt of the Red Guards and other pro-Mao "rebel leftists" to seize power from provincial and local "capitalist power-holders" of the Communist Party did not go smoothly in late December, 1966, and early January, 1967. During the same period, meanwhile, the outbursts of chaos, confusion, strikes, sabotages, factional struggles among the Maoist "revolution-ary" leftists, and armed clashes between anti-Mao and pro-Mao elements were widespread throughout the country.

In this difficult situation, Chairman Mao was compelled to turn to Defense Minister Lin Piao, his official heir apparent, and the armed forces, which had thus far maintained benign neutrality in the Cultural Revolution, to step in to render all-out support to the Maoist "proletarian revolutionaries."

The first official call for the 2.5 million men of the Chinese People's Liberation Army (PLA) to intervene throughout the country on the side of Maoist "revolutionaries" was given by the ruling Mao-Lin regime in Peking on January 23, 1967.[10] Through this call, Mao instructed the army to support the pro-Maoist "rebel" groups all over China, to break all anti-Maoist resistance—if necessary, by force—to do everything to guarantee the "regular functioning" of transport and industries and agricultural production, and to preserve law and order to avert the threat of an all-out civil war.[11] The same calls came again later. (At the same time, Chairman Mao instructed the Chinese people, including Maoist "revolutionary rebel" groups, to accept the authority of the army without question. This instruction was contained in an Eight-Point Order issued by the Military Affairs Committee under the Central Committee of the Chinese Communist Party on January 28, 1967, which specifically forbade the Red Guards and other Maoist "rebel" groups to undertake power seizures within the PLA under any circumstances.)[12]

Army intervention in the Cultural Revolution was the major factor in shifting the balance of power in China's internal power struggle in favor of the Maoist leftists and in ousting Mao's "revisionist" foes in the Party and government apparatus at all levels (provincial, county, municipal, and even down to the level of industrial enterprises and communes). With the demise of the old Party and government apparatus in all of China's twenty-nine provinces, special municipalities, and autonomous regions* in early 1967, local administrative power passed into the hands of the army—especially to the regional and district military commanders. The army also assumed many of the Party's former supervisory roles in the economic sphere.

By the spring of 1967, the leadership of Communist China had undergone the most extensive purge in the twenty-two-year history of the regime. Through wholesale purges, Mao had easily succeeded in virtually obliterating an organization which he had spent a lifetime creating. (The Party organizations within the army remained intact, however.) Government organizations also had been drastically affected at national, provincial, and local levels. At certain points, a significant por-

---

* The People's Republic of China or Communist China is divided into 29 major administrative units: 21 provinces, 5 autonomous regions, and 3 municipalities invested with a special status. (See *Table 2* and the attached map on Communist China.) For descriptive convenience, all of them will be hereafter called "provinces" in this book.

tion of the mainland was in a state of virtual anarchy. To count the major casualties only:[13] Of six men on the all-powerful Standing Committee of the Party Politburo (excluding Mao), only two, Defense Minister Lin Piao and Premier Chou En-lai, survived. Out of the thirteen members of the Party Politburo, seven members were purged, and only two of the six alternate Politburo members survived. Out of the ten members of the Party Secretariat, six members were purged, and four given other insignificant jobs. Of the active ninety-three full members of the Party's Central Committee, forty-eight were purged. Of the active seventy-nine alternate members of the Party's Central Committee, forty were purged (one member died in the hands of Red Guards, and another committed suicide), and twenty-nine were sharply criticized. Of the six regional Party bosses,[14] five were purged and one was demoted. (The demoted one was later rehabilitated.) The Chief Justice of the Supreme People's Court, Yang Hsiu-feng, committed suicide before he was attacked by Red Guards. Out of fourteen Deputy Premiers of the State Council (Cabinet), eight were purged. Out of seven members of the powerful Military Affairs Committee, three were purged. Mao's Cultural Revolution also hit the armed forces without exception. The purged victims of the army included: three out of seven vice-ministers of national defense; the Chief of General Staff and four of his eight deputies; the director and two out of five vice-directors of the powerful General Political Department; three of eight vice-commanders of the air force; the first political commissar of the navy; and the commanders of the armored force, the artillery, and the railway corps; and scores of regional military commanders and political commissars.[15] Hundreds of editors of central and local newspapers, writers, dozens of presidents and vice-presidents of the country's top universities and colleges, and also two vice-presidents and no fewer than fifteen key members of the Chinese Academy of Sciences were ousted. In short, Mao's extensive Cultural Revolution purge resulted in the creation of a leadership vacuum.

Mao Tse-tung's original idea in destroying the old Party-government apparatus was to replace it with a "truly" revolutionary government ("extensive democracy") modeled after the Paris Commune of 1871.[16] When that proved impractical in January, 1967,[17] the Maoist leadership introduced a new power structure to fill the vacuum: the Revolutionary Committee.[18] The Revolutionary Committee was to act as a provisional organ of power and administration across the country until the shattered apparatus of the Communist Party was rebuilt. Theoretically, the Committee was to be established on the basis of a "revolutionary triple alliance" consisting of (a) "revolutionary mass organizations" (i.e., Red Guards and other pro-Maoist "rebel" groups), (b) representatives of the army, and (c) remnants of the Party apparatus that still held official favor ("revolutionary cadres," i.e., pro-Maoist Party cadres or functionaries). At the provincial level, the Revolutionary Committees were to become the embodiment of the Maoist claim that a "seizure of power" on the "three-way alliance" principle had been accomplished. The army was to help the establishment of Revolutionary Committees throughout the country.

On January 31, 1967, Heilungkiang became the first province of Communist China to establish a Revolutionary Committee.[19] Its "seizure of power" on the "three-way coalition" was acclaimed by the Maoist leadership in Peking as a model to be emulated by all of Communist China's twenty-nine provinces.[20]

By the end of April, Heilungkiang's example was followed one after another by Shantung, Kweichow, Shanghai, Shansi, and Peking. The Revolutionary Committees in these six provinces and municipalities were characterized by the strong numerical representation of the Maoist "revolutionary rebels." (But some Maoist radicals in the top leadership of these committees were to lose power later.)

But twenty-three other provinces of Communist China failed to establish their own Revolutionary Committees during the first and second quarters of 1967, due chiefly to bitter and intense factional struggles among the Red Guards and other

Maoist groups for power, which will be discussed later. In those areas, the army established military control commissions and thereby assumed responsibility for exercising provisional leadership until new Revolutionary Committees were created.

Throughout 1966 and early 1967, Chairman Mao Tse-tung won most of the battles in his Cultural Revolution campaign. But he soon discovered, as his Cultural Revolution developed, that he had set in motion an extremely confused, complicated operation, whose consequences he could not foresee and, subsequently, control. What was more important, he had to compromise his original plan to meet unforeseen and uncontrollable contingencies.

For one thing, Mao discovered that the army was not solidly united behind Defense Minister Lin Piao, and was still divided by divergent regional allegiances, political nuances, personal loyalties, and professional aspirations. On July 24, and August 8, 1967, for example, Peking Radio admitted that early in 1967 the Cultural Revolution had little support both from the navy and the air force. It was disclosed in early 1967 that the army's response to Mao's orders of January 23, 1967, and thereafter was apparently motivated less by a conviction in the righteousness of Maoism or the Cultural Revolution than by the more common inclination of soldiers to impose stability on untidy situations in their country. During the six months following the army intervention in January, 1967, for example, the army supported a Maoist seizure of power actively in only the six provinces where the Revolutionary Committees were established by April, 1967.[21] (These six areas constituted the northeast base of Lin Piao's Fourth Field Army.)

In the rest of the twenty-three provinces, however, the army refused, in the words of Professor Allen S. Whiting, "to jump on the Maoist bandwagon." In fourteen or fifteen provinces the local army commanders adopted either benevolent or strict neutrality toward the Maoist revolutionary left while performing their duty to maintain law and order.[22] In these areas, the army sometimes found it necessary to suppress rampaging

Maoists as well as anti-Maoists for the sake of preserving law and order.[23] In ninè or ten provinces the local military commanders were coldly indifferent to Maoist leftists, merely minding their own business of restoring stability.[24] While the army in these twenty-three provinces did not execute Mao's orders in good faith, it stopped short of open defiance. Chairman Mao was still the father of the People's Republic of China, and there was a possibility of a U. S. attack on the Chinese mainland as a result of President Johnson's escalation of the Vietnam war in 1965.[25]

Moreover, the overwhelming majority of Mao's self-styled "revolutionary successors" were, contrary to Mao's optimistic expectation, corruptible youths and adults who were more inclined to win and enjoy power for themselves than to build a "true" Communist egalitarian society in China. During the course of the Cultural Revolution three articles written by Mao in the Yenan period were canonized as the "three constantly read articles." They are: "How Yu Kung Removed the Mountains" (a speech delivered by Mao to the Seventh National Congress of the Chinese Communist Party in June, 1945),[26] "Serve the People" (a speech delivered by Mao in 1944),[27] and "In Memory of Norman Bethune" (an essay written by Mao in 1939).[28] These three articles advanced the themes of the value of struggle, courage, and sacrifice, and especially the virtue of unselfishness.[29] But the Red Guards and other pro-Mao "rebel" groups did not live up to the Maoist version of new "Socialist" men who would voluntarily and enthusiastically sacrifice individualism for the sake of collectivistic goals. They had succeeded in the first task of destroying the old Party establishment dominated by Mao's "revisionist" opponents, but had failed in the second, and more important, task of constructing a "new revolutionary order" conceived by Chairman Mao.

Mao's Red Guards and other mass "revolutionary rebels" working in the provinces soon developed factions, which began to fight each other bitterly for division of the spoils and to engage in disputes over who genuinely represented the Cultural

Revolution and the Maoist ideology.[30] (For example, one Shanghai factory was split into over a hundred contending self-styled Maoist "rebel" factions.)[31] Vicious factionalism in the Maoist revolutionary leftist ranks, which arose as early as October, 1966, inevitably delayed the formation of the "revolutionary three-way alliance" in the twenty-three other provinces. They argued bitterly over which individuals and how many representatives from one faction as compared to another should be represented in the Revolutionary Committees. Factional struggles quickly degenerated into pitched battles, often using violence and arms, thereby discrediting the Cultural Revolution badly.

What was worse, the Maoists proved inadequate replacements for the purged or denounced Party-government bureaucrats because they lacked knowledge of government and administration even at the lowest level. Therefore, it was necessary for the army, which lacked governmental experience and administrative skills, to reinstate many of the old Party and government officials ousted in the early purges of the Cultural Revolution, even though they were reluctant to resume their old posts. Needing the help of experienced officials, army commanders in many provinces, with the approval of the Proletarian Headquarters in Peking, tried to bring many old Party cadres into the Revolutionary Committees.[32]

The reemergence of these old Party veterans angered the Red Guards and other pro-Maoists who were briefly catapulted into power by the Cultural Revolution. The Maoists were dead opposed to the army policy of rehabilitating the anti-Mao Party-government bureaucrats, since this meant a betrayal of the aim of the Cultural Revolution and the usurpation of their newly won power by their discredited foes—"restoration of the old." So they clamored for renewed purges of the veteran Party and government officials previously purged or labeled "counter-revolutionaries," and even accused the army of harboring "capitalist power-holders."

From the very outset of the active military intervention, in short, the principal characteristic of the Cultural Revolution in the spring of 1967 was increased antagonism and hostility between the army and the Maoist revolutionary left in a great number of Communist China's twenty-nine provinces, rooted in their conflicting objectives and interests. Mao's repeated pleas for mutual trust and cooperation between them[33] did not help the situation.

Furthermore, the interests of regional military commanders in maintaining law and order invariably came into conflict with the rampant and unprincipled factional movement of the Red Guards and other pro-Maoists. By virtue of the proliferation of Maoist revolutionary "rebel" factions and organizations in the course of the Cultural Revolution, and because every "rebel" faction claimed to be loyal to Chairman Mao and his Cultural Revolution, it was difficult for the local army commanders, as Lin Piao later acknowledged in his political report to the Ninth Party Congress of April, 1969,[34] to check their Maoist credentials and to distinguish the genuine Maoist from the sham Maoist groups. During the first and second quarters of 1967, local military commanders had not been provided by Mao with objective criteria to distinguish "genuine proletarian revolutionaries" from false ones, and the instructions they did receive were usually too general and even contradictory to be helpful. They resented the Mao-Lin command in Peking for not having sufficiently appreciated their plight in dealing with factionalism in the ranks of the Maoist revolutionary left, and for giving too much freedom to the Red Guards and other groups at the great expense of law and order.

Fearing that unprincipled factionalism within the Red Guard and other mass "revolutionary" segments of the Maoist three-way alliance would lead the country to anarchism, army commanders in many provinces chose to support one faction (usually moderate or conservative) over others (usually radical), primarily in the interest of rapidly restoring order, rather than on the basis of the Thought of Mao Tse-tung or directives from Chairman Mao and Defense Minister Lin Piao. In some provinces, the army used its muscle to suppress Red Guards and other mass "rebel" groups to restore peace.[35]

This touched off an appeal for a purge of the army by the Maoist revolutionary leftists (usually radical elements), who had close connections with the radical faction of the Maoist leadership in Peking (i.e., the Cultural Revolution Group under the Central Committee of the Chinese Communist Party) but who were suppressed by, or out of favor with, the local military commanders. Instead of supporting army commanders for forming "revolutionary three-way alliance," these radical Maoists launched bitter attacks against local military control commissions for failure to support them actively. Reacting to this attack, the local military commanders had opened fire on the attacking radical Maoist "rebel" factions in self-defense and suppressed or arrested them as "counter-revolutionary reactionaries."[36]

As expected, local military commanders and the Maoist Proletarian Headquarters in Peking, especially its radical faction led by Chiang Ching (Mme. Mao) and Chen Po-ta, experienced considerable friction and discord over the question of which "rebel" group was the "true revolutionary." In fact, many local army commanders were transferred or disgraced for failing or neglecting to support the "genuine" Maoist "rebels" in favor of the "wrong" factions.[37] (The conflict between the Maoist faction in Peking and the local army commanders culminated dramatically in the Wuhan incident of July, 1967, to be discussed later.)

Ever since Mao Tse-tung launched the Cultural Revolution, the pervasive factionalism among the Maoist "rebels" had been one of the major issues dividing the Maoist leadership in Peking. The radical faction within the leadership had acquired a vested interest in, and an emotional commitment to, continuing the turmoil for the enhancement of its power status, and had endorsed unrestricted "proletarian" factional activity as an essential part of "uninterrupted class struggle" to achieve the objectives of the Cultural Revolution. But the moderate faction, led by Premier Chou En-lai and senior military commanders, had become alarmed at the anarchic deterioration of law and order, and had sought to impose a modicum of civil order on the nation by limiting the factional activities of the Maoist "rebels." (The Maoist leadership in Peking during the Cultural Revolution can be described as an uneasy two-way alliance, and the consequent tug of war, between moderate and radical factions, with neither of them gaining total ascendancy. As will be seen later in this book, Chairman Mao has remained in the center of these factions to keep them working together, but has also manipulated them to serve his own political purpose.)

During the first and second quarters of 1967, the radical faction led by Chiang Ching had been dominant in the Maoist policy-making council in Peking. In its view, the army, especially local army commanders, had gone too far in the direction of order and stability, and it advocated a more militant policy in support of the Maoist revolutionary extremists.[38] It was disenchanted with the performance of the army in the spring of 1967, especially its policy of indiscriminately rehabilitating many old Party-government cadres formerly purged by the Maoist revolutionary left as anti-Maoist "demons and freaks," while suppressing the "genuine" (i.e., radical) Maoist rebels at the same time. Therefore, it instructed the Maoist radicals in mid-March, 1967 to escalate poster attacks on the military for assuming too much authority, for acting too roughly, and for suppressing them harshly. What was more important, it succeeded in issuing the April 6, 1967, Military Affairs Committee Ten-Point Directive which sharply curtailed the authority of the army to intervene in factional strife among the Red Guards and other Maoist groups.[39] More specifically, this new directive, which considerably modified the January 28, 1967, Eight-Point Order of the Military Affairs Committee,[40] prohibited the army's opening fire on, or using force against, the Maoist revolutionary organizations, suppressing or arresting them as "counter-revolutionaries," and taking any other "important" actions towards them without first receiving instructions from the Mao-Lin "proletarian" command in Peking.[41] The new directive also instructed local army commanders to "rectify immediately" all of their previous errors in dealing with the Maoist revolutionary radicals, releasing all those previously arrested, reinstating all those formerly labeled counter-revolutionary reactionaries, and carrying out self-criticism for their "wrong" conduct.[42] (But the Maoist revolutionary "rebels" were later warned again not to fight with, or use force against, the army.)[43] By and large, the net effect of the April 6, 1967, directive was to handcuff the army at the very critical moment it was ordered to maintain law and order and also to take over the governmental responsibility of running and administering the troubled country.

As a result of leashing the army while unleashing the Maoist "revolutionary rebels," intense, costly, and violent strife among the Maoist "rebel" factions began again in earnest throughout the country, culminating in the Wuhan incident of July, 1967. For example, according to Professor Chalmers A. Johnson, "four hundred rebels were said to have been burned alive in a multi-story building in Chengchow, Honan."[44] For the second quarter of 1967 the participants in these factional struggles used poles, daggers, small arms, automatic weapons, mortars, artillery, and even tanks and armored cars in rare instances. Looting, murder, robbery, immorality, workers' strikes and desertions, arms thefts, profiteering, and black markets were widespread by the end of August, 1967. As the internal disorders intensified, the Mao-Lin leadership in Peking issued a new directive on June 6, 1967 which once again emphasized the army's responsibility for maintaining law and order,[45] but it came too late.

The incident of mid-July, 1967, in which the local army commander in the Wuhan Military Region revolted against Mao by arresting two important emissaries from Peking, was a turning point toward moderation in the Cultural Revolution.

To tell the Wuhan incident briefly:[46] In the vital industrial city of Wuhan there were two major "rebel" factions claiming to represent Maoism. One was called the Three Steels, a 400,000-

strong radical coalition of steel workers and college students, favored by the Maoist (especially the radical) leadership in Peking. The other was the One Million Heroes, a "conservative" coalition of 300,000 factory workers, public security employees, and former trade-union leaders, favored by the Wuhan Military Regional Command under General Ch'en Tsai-tao. Factional struggle between the two was brutal, and the Three Steels was suffering a defeat because of the local army's support of the One Million Heroes. On July 16, 1967, Chairman Mao's two important representatives—Public Security Minister Hsieh Fu-chih and Wang Li, a member of the Cultural Revolution Group and propaganda boss of the Maoist camp—arrived in Wuhan to mediate the factional conflicts there in favor of Peking's favored Three Steels. The two emissaries delivered an order from Peking instructing the army not to support the One Million Heroes. What was more important, the leaders of the Wuhan Military Region were then ordered to admit their "mistakes" by carrying out public self-criticism before the Maoist revolutionary leftists. Infuriated, General Ch'en Tsai-tao and his loyal soldiers kidnapped, manhandled, and publicly humiliated the two emissaries. (Hsieh's secretary was said to have been stabbed to death. Wang Li's leg was said to have been broken.) The two representatives were released on July 22, 1967, possibly because of the movement of five warships and paratroops near the city for a prompt release, or possibly because of the diplomatic intervention of Premier Chou En-lai. A few weeks later, General Ch'en was fired and General Tseng Ssu-yü took over as Commander in Wuhan, and the army then began to support the Three Steels.

Immediately after the Wuhan incident, some ultra-leftist elements (including Mme. Mao) in the Maoist leadership in Peking decided to exploit the incident to further their own goals by laying all the blame for failures and setbacks of the Cultural Revolution on the law-and-order-oriented army. Regarding the army as untrustworthy for the cause of the Cultural Revolution, they attacked the "capitalist power-holders" within the army and advocated the extension of the purge into the armed forces,[47] thereby precipitating a short-lived (late July–August) ultra-leftist phase of the Cultural Revolution. In unprecedently shrill and incendiary language, they urged the Red Guards and other Maoist revolutionary extremists to "take up arms" against, and strike back at, the military and to "drag out the handful of capitalist-roaders in the army" throughout the country, something from which the army had hitherto been exempt.[48]

When the Cultural Revolution entered this ultra-leftist phase, the unity of the Chinese People's Liberation Army, which Defense Minister Lin Piao had tried to keep at least outwardly intact, was seriously threatened. Although Mao Tse-tung and Lin Piao managed to purge a number of high-ranking military leaders and regional and local army commanders in the early phase of the Cultural Revolution, the threat of erupting disunity in the armed forces led them to turn against the ultra-leftist extremists.

Mao and Lin Piao knew perfectly well that the 2.5-million-man army, so far relatively untouched by the Cultural Revolution, was the only nationally effective and comparatively unified force remaining in Communist China in 1967 that had the organization and power to stop the steamroller of the Cultural Revolution or even challenge the ruling Mao-Lin faction in Peking effectively. In fact, they were at that time taking measures to insure the political loyalty of the armed forces. In the summer of 1967, the Maoist press said bluntly: "It is imperative for the proletariat [i.e., the Maoist "revolutionary rebels"] to take firm hold of the gun and keep a firm hold of the army. . . . Should the army be lost and its power usurped by bad elements, then everything achieved by the proletariat and the working people will come to naught."[49] But the army's patience with unbridled factional strife among the revolutionary leftists was running short, and the ultra-leftist phase of the

Cultural Revolution provoked the army, acting in self-defense, to force the ouster of ultra-leftist leaders in the Maoist camp in Peking. In short, Mao and Lin could not afford to antagonize the army further by extending the purge into it, and decided to side with the army against the ultra-leftist leaders.

At the same time, Mao and Lin wanted to call a halt to the destructive phase of the Cultural Revolution, recognizing the gravity of the situation in China. Considering the seriousness of the crisis in the summer of 1967, it was necessary and even tactically convenient for Mao, as Philip Bridgham astutely observes, "to sacrifice a number of prominent [ultra-leftist] members of the Cultural Revolution Group, holding them, rather than the policies they were administering [under his personal guidance], responsible for the nation-wide disturbance in China."[50]

In August, 1967, key members of the extreme leftist group in the Maoist leadership in Peking (e.g., Wang Li, Kuan Feng, Lin Chieh, and Mu Hsin), all of whom were members of the Cultural Revolution Group under the Central Committee of the Chinese Communist Party, were accused of being Kuomintang (Nationalist) agents and purged. (Peking wall posters referred to them as "counter-revolutionary turtle eggs."[51] "Turtle egg" means "bastard" in Chinese usage.) But Mme. Mao was saved from the purge apparently because of her personal relation to Chairman Mao. On September 5, 1967, she perhaps found herself compelled to pay tribute to the role of the military in the Cultural Revolution, condemned the attacks upon it, and asked her followers to restrain themselves.[52] Mao's special Cultural Revolution Group, created to guide his Cultural Revolution campaign in late 1966, was considerably weakened (see *Table 1*). The publication of *Hung Ch'i*, which had become the principal organ of the Maoist radicals and the pacesetter in the attacks on the military, was temporarily suspended in November, 1967. At the same time, the Maoist press condemned "ultra-leftism" or "anarchism" as the "most serious danger" to Communist China.[53] This drive against "ultra-leftism" was also

Table 1: *The Cultural Revolution Group under the Central Committee of the Chinese Communist Party (set up right after the Central Committee's Eleventh Plenum of August, 1966.)*

Abbreviations: CC—Central Committee; CCP—Chinese Communist Party; PLA—People's Liberation Army

Original Members	Positions Held in August 1966	
1) CHEN Po-ta	Politburo member of CC, CCP; Editor-in-Chief of *Red Flag* (Hung Ch'i).	
2) CHIANG Ch'ing (Mme. Mao)		
3) KANG Sheng	Politburo member of CC, CCP.	
4) YAO Wen-yuan	Editor-in-Chief of Shanghai *Liberation Daily*.	
5) CHANG Chun-chiao	Secretary of Secretariat of CCP Shanghai Municipal Committee.	
6) LIU Chih-chien	Deputy Director of PLA Political Dept.	(purged in January/February 1967)
7) TAO Chu	First Secretary of CCP Central-South China Bureau.	(purged in January/February 1967)
8) CHANG Ping-hua	First Secretary of CCP Hunan Provincial Committee; CCP Deputy Director of Propaganda.	(purged in January/February 1967)
9) WANG Jen-chung	First Secretary of CCP Hupeh Provincial Committee.	(purged in January/February 1967)
10) CHI Pen-yu	*Red Flag* editorial staff.	(purged in January/February 1967)

Table 1: The Cultural Revolution Group under the Central Committee of the Chinese Communist Party (set up right after the Central Committee's Eleventh Plenum of August, 1966.) (Continued)

Abbreviations: CC—Central Committee; CCP—Chinese Communist Party; PLA—People's Liberation Army

Original Members		Positions Held in August 1966
11) KUAN Feng	(purged in September/ October 1967)	Red Flag editorial staff.
12) WANG Li	(purged in August 1967)	Red Flag editorial staff.
13) MU Hsin	(purged in September/ October 1967)	Editor of Kuangming Daily.
14) HSIEH Tang-chung	(purged in January/ February 1967)	PLA Cultural Affairs Director.
15) LIU Wei-chien	(purged in January/ February 1967)	Propaganda Chief of CCP Southwest China Bureau.
16) YANG Chih-lin	(purged in January/ February 1967)	First Secretary of CCP Tsinghai Provincial Committee.
17) CHENG Chi-chiao	(purged in January/ February 1967)	Propaganda Chief of CCP Northeast China Bureau.
18) LIN Chieh	(purged in September/ October 1967)	Deputy Editor of Red Flag.

undoubtedly aimed at the Red Guards and other Maoist "rebels" who refused to end their factional violence and lawlessness and to submit themselves to discipline.

After the Wuhan incident and the purge of the ultra-leftists, the direction of the Cultural Revolution had come under the aegis of the moderates led by Premier Chou En-lai and a group of senior army officers rather than the radicals. At the same time, the new turn toward moderation led to the brief eclipse of Chiang Ching, the leader of the radical wing in the Maoist camp in Peking.

NOTES TO CHAPTER 2

1. See, for example, *Jen-min Jih-pao*, June 8, 1966; and "Circular of the Central Committee of the Communist Party of China," May 16, 1966, *New China News Agency*, Peking, May 16, 1967.

2. This statement was made by Mao on December 21, 1939. See *Current Background*, American Consulate General, Hong Kong, No. 891, October 8, 1969, p. 10.

3. See *Hung Ch'i*, December 13, 1966; and *Jen-min Jih-pao*, December 26, 1966. See also Lin Piao's report to the Ninth Congress of the Chinese Communist Party, delivered on April 1 and adopted on April 14, 1969, reprinted in *Peking Review*, Special Issue, April 28, 1909, pp. 19–20.

4. See *Jen-min Jih-pao*, January 9, 12, 20, and 25, 1967; *New China News Agency*, January 14, and 25, 1967; *Chieh-fang-chün Pao*, January 12, 1967; *Hung Ch'i*, January 12, 1967; *Shanghai Wen Hui Pao*, January 20, 1967; *Peking Radio*, January 16, 1967; *Moscow Radio*, January 14, 1967; and *The China Quarterly*, April–June, 1967, pp. 202–204.

5. Chalmers A. Johnson, "China: The Cultural Revolution in Structural Perspective," *Asian Survey*, January 1968, p. 6.

6. See footnote 4.

7. *Jen-min Jih-pao*, July 22, 1966; October 31, 1966; and January 30, 1967. See also *Yomiuri Shimbun*, Tokyo, November 7, 1966.

8. Chalmers Johnson, *op. cit.*, p. 6.

9. *Jen-min Jih-pao*, December 26, 1966.

10. "The People's Liberation Army Firmly Backs the Proletarian Revolutionaires," *Chienh-fang-chün Pao*, January 25, 1967; *New China News Agency*, January 25, 1967.

11. *Ibid.*

12. This was disclosed by Chiang Ching (Mme. Mao Tse-tung) on April 20, 1967. See *Jen-min Jih-pao,* April 21, 1967.

13. This writer would not contend that the following statistics on the major casualties of the Cultural Revolution should be considered absolutely correct. For different statistical data on the major casualties of Mao's Cultural Revolution see Charles Neuhauser, "The Impact of the Cultural Revolution on the Chinese Communist Party Machine," *Asian Survey,* June 1968, p. 466; Jürgen Domes, "The Cultural Revolution and the Army," *Asian Survey,* May 1968, pp. 360–363; Donald Klein, "The State Council and the Cultural Revolution," *The China Quarterly,* July–September, 1968, pp. 78–95, and Parris H. Chang, "Mao's Great Purge: A Political Balance Sheet," *Problems of Communism,* March–April, 1969, pp. 1–10.

14. Communist China created 6 regional bureaus of the Chinese Communist Party in 1961 as links between the Party hierarchy and lower echelons of the country.

15. Jürgen Domes, *op. cit.,* p. 362. See also *What's Happening on the Chinese Mainland,* Taipei, Taiwan, March 8, 1970.

16. See The Decisions of the Central Committee of the Chinese Communist Party concerning the Cultural Revolution adopted on August 8, 1966, reprinted in *Peking Review,* August 12, 1966, pp. 6–11. (Point 9)

17. The idea of the Paris Commune was officially written off by Mao on February 23, 1967. *Shanghai Radio,* February 24, 1967. See also *Yomiuri Shimbun,* Tokyo, February 19, 1967.

18. See *Jen-min Jih-pao,* February 2 and 10, 1967; and *Hung Ch'i,* March 9 and 10, 1967.

19. *Jen-min Jih-pao,* February 2 and 10, 1967. See also *Current Scene,* Hong Kong, June 1, 1968, pp. 1–12.

20. *Ibid.*

21. Jürgen Domes, *op. cit.,* p. 356. See also Jürgen Domes, "The Role of the Military in the Formation of Revolutionary Committees 1967–68," *The China Quarterly,* October–December 1970, pp. 116–132.

22. *Ibid.* See also *Chieh-fang-chün Pao,* January 25, 1967; and February 26, 1967.

23. *Ibid.*

24. *Ibid.*

25. For an interesting study of how the United States almost went to war with Communist China over Vietnam see Allen S. Whiting, "How We Almost Went to War with China," *Look* (Magazine), April 29, 1969, pp. 76–79.

26. Mao Tse-tung, *Selected Works* (New York: International Publishers, 1956), Vol. IV, pp. 316–318.

27. *Ibid.,* pp. 219–220.

28. *Ibid.,* Vol. III (1954), pp. 104–106.

29. For the detailed discussion of the values expounded by Mao Tse-tung in these three articles see Maurice Meisner, "Utopian Goals and

Ascetic Values in Chinese Communist Ideology," *The Journal of Asian Studies*, November 1968, pp. 101–110.

30. For a detailed study of Maoist factionalism in the Cultural Revolution see "Mass Factionalism in Communist China," *Current Scene*, May 15, 1968, pp. 1–13. For example, by January 24, 1967, 111 "rebel" groups had been reported in Shanghai, 54 in Wuhan, 87 in Kiangsi, 42 in Chinghai and 300 in Lhasa. *The China Quarterly*, No. 30 (April–June 1967), p. 217. See also *Jen-min Jih-pao*, May 22, 1967; May 25, 1967; *Shanghai Wen Hui Pao*, May 25 and 26, 1967; *Chieh-fang-chün Pao*, February 13, 1967; *Jen-min Jih-pao*, February 26, 1967; *Hung Ch'i*, February 13, 1967; and *Shanghai Wen Hui Pao*, April 29, 1967.

31. See "The 'January Revolution' Experience in Shanghai," Canton, *Kuang-yin Hung-ch'i* (Canton Printing Red Flag), No. 2, November 23, 1967, in *Survey of China Mainland Press*, Hong Kong, American Consulate-General, No. 4145, March 25, 1968.

32. The Decision of the Central Committee of the Chinese Communist Party Concerning the Great Proletarian Cultural Revolution, adopted on August 8, 1966, said that most Party cadres were "good and comparatively good." See *Peking Review*, August 12, 1966, p. 9. The same theme was restated on February 20, 1967, by the letter of the Central Committee of the Chinese Communist Party to poor and lower-middle peasants and cadres at all levels in rural people's communes. See *New China News Agency*, February 20, 1967. For the same Maoist appeal for the proper and mild treatment of cadres see *New China News Agency*, February 22, 1966; and *Peking Review*, March 3, 1967, pp. 5–9.

33. An editorial in the April 27, 1967 issue of *Hung Ch'i* stressed the need for closer ties between the army and the Maoist "rebels." "Warmly Respond to the Call to Support the Army and Cherish the People," *Hung Ch'i*, April 27, 1967.

34. *Peking Review*, Special Issue, April 28, 1969, p. 18.

35. Charles Neuhauser, *op. cit.*, p. 479.

36. Philip Bridgham, "Mao's Cultural Revolution: Origin and Development," *The China Quarterly*, January–March 1967, p. 16.

37. They were army commanders in the military districts of Anhwei, Chekiang, Honan, Kirin, and Fukien, and in the military regions of Inner Mongolia, Chengtu, Peking, Kuming, and Wuhan. See Parris H. Chang, "The Revolutionary Committee in China; Two Case Studies: Heilungkiang and Honan," *Current Scene*, June 1, 1968, p. 19.

38. "On the Revolutionary Three-in-One Combination," *Hung Ch'i*, March 9, 1967.

39. *Jen-min Jih-pao*, April 21, 1967; and *Yomiuri Shimbun*, April 6 and 9, 1967.

40. See footnote 12 of this chapter.

41. See footnote 39 of this chapter.

42. *Ibid.*

43. *Hung Ch'i*, May 8, 1967.

44. Quoted from Chalmers Johnson, *op. cit.*, p. 10.

45. *The CCP Documents of the Great Proletarian Cultural Revolution 1966–67*, Union Research Institute, Hong Kong, 1968, pp. 463–464.

46. For detailed accounts of the Wuhan incident see *Sankei*, Tokyo, September 29 and 30, 1967; *Mainichi Shimbun*, Tokyo, August 1, 1967; and *The China Quarterly*, October–December 1967, pp. 185–190.

47. *Hung Ch'i*, July 31 and August 17, 1967. See also *Jen-min Jih-pao*, September 8, 1967.

48. *Sankei*, August 22, 1967; *Radio Peking*, July 30, 1967; "On Military Power," *Canton Hung-se Pao-tung* (Red Riot), August 1, 1967, in the *Survey of the China Mainland Press* (SCMP), No. 4701, pp. 13–17; and "Comment on 'On Military Power'," *Canton Wu-i-wu Chun-pao* (May 15 Combat Bulletin), September 29, 1967, in *SCMP*, No. 4068, pp. 16–19.

49. *Hung Ch'i*, July 31, 1967.

50. Quoted from Philip Bridgham, *op. cit.*, p. 27.

51. Stanley Karnow's dispatch in *The Washington Post*, March 4, 1968, p. 15.

52. For the full text of her speech see *The China Quarterly*, October–December 1967, pp. 212–216.

53. See *Jen-min Jih-pao*, September 8, 1967; *Shanghai Wen Hui Pao*, October 21, 1967; and February 6, 1968.

CHAPTER 3

The Cultural Revolution
in Retreat

IN THE SUMMER of 1967, Mao's Cultural Revolution in fact brought so much turmoil, confusion, economic and social chaos, intense and vicious factional strife, and anarchy that Chairman Mao had to make new efforts to bring his Cultural Revolution under control and to restore domestic tranquility.

It is not known whether Mao and his loyal supporters chose to curb the more radical, unruly aspects of the Cultural Revolution, or were forced to do so by regional military pressure. From August, 1967, on, at any rate, new trends toward moderation became discernible, particularly following Mao's trip in September, 1967, to a number of provinces where serious disturbances had occurred. It seems likely that Mao was persuaded by his military commanders to go and see for himself how things had deteriorated in China since his Cultural Revolution started in 1966.

After September, 1967, factionalism was condemned by the Maoist press as a "crime"[1] and the factional activities of the Maoist revolutionary leftists were curbed. On September 5, 1967, the central leadership in Peking issued a highly important order which urged competing leftist factions to stop fighting among themselves, called upon them to support the army, firmly forbade attacks upon it, and decreed that all weapons previously seized or stolen from the military be returned.[2] Most importantly, the army was authorized to take a firmer hand with, or start disciplinary action against, the Red Guards and other Maoist mass "rebel" groups in the provinces, and also given a mandate to keep peace. (More specifically, the army was for the first time permitted to "hit back in self-defense," but only if and when attacked by the Maoist revolutionary leftists. It was again specifically forbidden by Chairman Mao to suppress the Maoist "rebel" organizations by involving itself in Maoist factional struggles.)[3] The Maoist leadership in Peking called for unity among rival Maoist factions, re-emphasized the new mild cadre policy of rehabilitating formerly purged or disgraced Party and government officials,[4] and assigned to the army the main responsibility of helping the expeditious establishment of the new provincial power structure—the Revolutionary Committees which were based on the so-called "three-way alliance."[5] One of Chairman Mao's important instructions during his September, 1967, tour was that the process of setting up the committees in all the twenty-nine provinces of China be speeded up and completed by the end of January, 1968.

Throughout the fall and winter of 1967, the Chinese People's Liberation Army made great efforts to restore peace and order and tighten control over unruly and protesting Maoist factions. The army sent the Maoist "rebels" back to the schools and factories, reopened the schools with army political commissars on hand to supervise both the instruction and the ex-Red Guard pupils at schools,[6] enforced strict discipline against troublemakers, and exerted great pressure on rival Maoist factional groups to conclude the "revolutionary three-way alliance" or establish Revolutionary Committees as new instruments of local power. It also took over the tasks of directing industry, supervising agriculture, and overseeing rail and road transportation throughout the country. In its effort to clean up the wreckage of the Cultural Revolution, the 2.5-million-man army has since September, 1967, practically taken over the running of Communist China.

But the army lacked the skill to repair the extensive political, economic, and social damage caused by Mao's radical Cultural Revolution. Therefore, many of the country's old-line Party and government officials and managerial experts who were pushed aside during the height of the Cultural Revolution had to be rehabilitated. A face-saving pretext offered by the Maoist leadership and press was that the majority of the dismissed Party and government officials were "good or comparatively good" and must be allowed to "stand out" or become rehabilitated.[7]

By May, 1968, the provincial-level Revolutionary Committees had been formally established in twenty-four of the country's twenty-nine provinces.[8] (See *Table 2*.) Peking had not been able to organize the Committees in the border areas, such as Tibet, Sinkiang, Yunnan, Fukien, and Kiangsi. Except for the first half-dozen (set up "spontaneously" in early 1967 by the Maoist revolutionary leftists), nearly all of the Revolutionary Committees had been formed after long negotiations in Peking involving representatives of local Maoist "rebel" factions, and of central and local authorities, including the army. It appears that Peking made the most concessions, such as allowing local (army) authorities to determine the composition and political complexion of the provincial-level Revolutionary Committees.[9]

The majority of the provincial-level Revolutionary Committees established after August, 1967, were in fact dominated by the military—the strongest pillar of the "triple alliance."[10] (It is also accurate to say that these committees were more of a double alliance than a triple alliance, with the Red Guards and other Maoist mass "rebel" groups only tolerated by the more powerful military and unpurged Party cadres.) To put it another way, the majority of the provincial-level Revolutionary Committees established between August, 1967, and May, 1968, had become more than a façade for direct military administration. What was more important, they were dominated by more

conservative or moderate army representatives, suggesting the
enhanced power of the moderate faction in the Maoist leadership in Peking.[11] (See the *map*, page 50, *Table 2* and *Appendix
II.*)

Table 2: Principal Administrative Divisions of Communist China

Province and / or Military District	Military Region*	Dates of Establishment of Revolutionary Committees
1. Heilungkiang	Shenyang	January 31, 1967
2. Kirin		March 6, 1968
3. Liaoning		March 10, 1968
*4. Inner Mongolian Autonomous Region	Inner Mongolia	November 1, 1967
5. Hopeh	Peking	February 3, 1968
6. Peking Municipality		April 20, 1967
7. Tientsin Municipality		December 6, 1967
8. Shansi		March 18, 1967
*9. Shantung	Tsinan	February 23, 1967
10. Kiangsu	Nanking	March 23, 1968
11. Shanghai Municipality		February 5, 1967
12. Anhwei		April 18, 1968
13. Chekiang		March 24, 1968
14. Fukien	Foochow	August 19, 1968
15. Kiangsi		January 5, 1968
16. Honan	Wuhan	January 27, 1968
17. Hupeh		February 5, 1968
18. Hunan	Canton	April 9, 1968
19. Kwangtung		February 21, 1968
20. Kwangsi Chuang Autonomous Region		August 26, 1968
21. Shensi	Lanchow	May 1, 1968
22. Ningsia Hui Autonomous Region		April 10, 1968
23. Kansu		January 24, 1968
24. Tsinghai		August 12, 1967

Table 2: Principal Administrative Divisions of
Communist China (Continued)

Province and / or Military District	Military Region*	Dates of Establishment of Revolutionary Committees
*25. Sinkiang Uighur Autonomous Region	Sinkiang	September 5, 1968
*26. Szechwan	Chengtu	May 31, 1968
27. Kweichow	Kunming	February 14, 1967
28. Yunnan		August 13, 1968
*29. Tibetan Autonomous Region	Tibet	September 5, 1968

* In five cases the province is also the military region. When the military region comprises two or more provinces, each province is then constituted as a military district. Hainan Island is the only military district below provincial size.

But the spread of the Revolutionary Committees throughout the country did not signify that law and order were really being restored in China. The course of their formation was marked by tension and conflicts, continuing in most cases after the new "three-way alliance" institutions were formed. (Premier Chou En-lai often had to dictate truces or "agreements" to disputing Maoist "rebel" factions concerning the formation of the Revolutionary Committees.) In many provinces, as said previously, the Revolutionary Committees were dominated by military leaders. But as the military were often outsiders—busy officers with other duties to perform—the real conflict for power had developed between radical (leftist) and moderate (conservative) elements from both the Red Guards and other pro-Mao mass "rebel" organizations. The army, forbidden by Mao to use force against or to suppress the Maoist revolutionary left by involving itself in Maoist factional strifes,[12] frequently found it practical or convenient to stand aside and let the Maoist "rebel" factions fight it out.

Though in general the radical and moderate elements within the ranks of the Maoist revolutionary left had taken their bitter

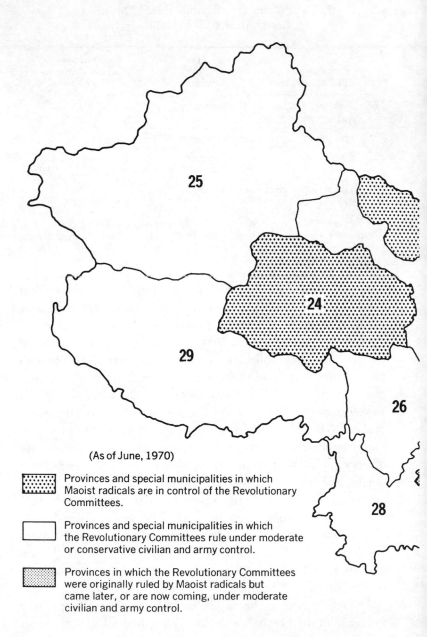

(As of June, 1970)

Provinces and special municipalities in which Maoist radicals are in control of the Revolutionary Committees.

Provinces and special municipalities in which the Revolutionary Committees rule under moderate or conservative civilian and army control.

Provinces in which the Revolutionary Committees were originally ruled by Maoist radicals but came later, or are now coming, under moderate civilian and army control.

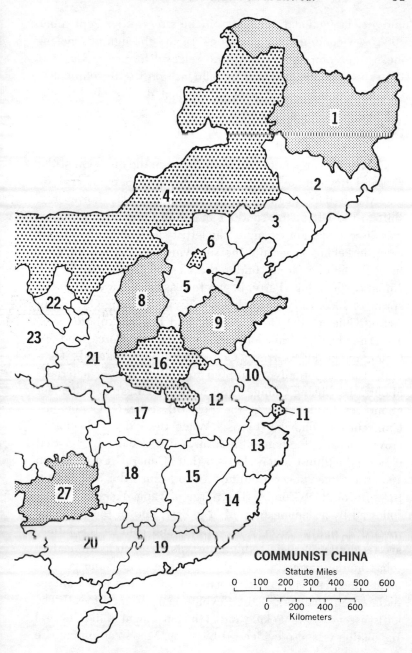

COMMUNIST CHINA

Statute Miles

0   100   200   300   400   500   600

0   200   400   600
Kilometers

and vicious factional struggles off the streets after September 1967, they continued their factional rivalry through less violent means (i.e., propaganda wars and selected terror or assassination) for positions of power or influence on the Revolutionary Committees which were being established at all levels throughout the country, from the level of provinces and special municipalities down to Hsien (counties) and social and economic enterprises and schools.[13]

The period of restraint and moderation in the direction of the Cultural Revolution had continued between September 1967 and March 1968. Beginning in early March, 1968, however, a shift to the left in the conduct of Mao's Cultural Revolution was discernible. For example, the leftist elements in the Maoist camp in Peking, especially the surviving members of the Cultural Revolution Group under the Central Committee of the Chinese Communist Party, began to reassert themselves in the spring of 1968. In late March 1968, "General" Yang Cheng-wu, Acting Chief of the General Staff, and his two subordinates, Yu Lin-chin, Political Commissar of the Air Force, and Fu Chung-pi, Peking Garrison Commander, were purged. "General" Yang reportedly attempted to collect "black materials" about Miss Chiang Ching,[14] and made a derogatory statement about her sudden rise in the political scene of Communist China in the following terms: "When the old hen begins to crow at sunrise, the honorable farmyard is in danger."[15] A Red Guard tabloid in Canton charged that "General" Fu in March 1968 tried to engineer a military coup against the Party's Cultural Revolution Group.[16] The purge of Yang, Yu, and Fu was followed by a denunciation of "rightists" and of the tendency toward "a rightist reversal of verdicts and counter-revolutionary restoration"—that is, the army's policy of indiscriminately rehabilitating formerly purged or dismissed Party and government bureaucrats at a great expense of the Maoist leftist groups within the framework of the Revolutionary Committees.[17] The leftist ascendancy in Peking and in the movement of the Cultural Revolution was also evidenced by Mme. Mao's continuing rise in public prominence and power in 1968. For example, the slogan "Learn from Comrade Chiang Ching" appeared, and in the 1968 May Day celebration in Peking, she was placed in the ninth leadership position instead of nineteenth as she had been on October 1, 1967.

Another significant manifestation of the shift to the left in the spring of 1968 was the Maoist press attitude toward factionalism. As late as February, 1968, factionalism was condemned as a "crime," but after March 1968 the Maoist press said that there was such a thing as good factionalism. More specifically, the Maoist press said that "bourgeois factionalism" was bad and to be condemned, but "proletarian factionalism" was good, so it had to be upheld.[18] "Rightism" was defined as the gravest danger to Communist China, instead of the previous contention that "ultra-leftism" and "anarchism" were the worst problems. The virtue of the Red Guards, rather than their faults, was stressed in provincial newspapers. In June 1968, the Maoist press bluntly called the suppression of the Maoist radicals a "bourgeois crime."[19] In the same month, a radical Maoist newspaper in Shanghai demanded that the Maoist revolutionary leftists be "given a free hand in carrying out [proletarian factional] struggles."[20] Some provincial propaganda organs, which always reflected the radical views of Chiang Ching and her Cultural Revolution Group members, also urged that "a handful of renegades, spies, counter-revolutionaries, capitalist- roaders and other bad elements be dragged out" of the thousands of revolutionary committees that now constituted the control apparatus in China.

The most plausible explanation for the shift to the left in the direction of the Cultural Revolution in the spring of 1968 seems to be that the leftist leaders in the Maoist camp in Peking had continued to fight for their views even after their temporary eclipse in the fall of 1967 and, through Chiang Ching's strong influence on her husband, Chairman Mao, moved in early 1968 to take corrective measures to counter the growing strength in the provinces of elements unsympathetic or even hostile to the

Cultural Revolution's premises and objectives. The radical Maoist leaders in Peking may have feared that the period of moderation had gone too far, and that if what they denounced as a tendency toward "a rightist reversal of verdicts and counter-revolutionary restoration" continued unchecked, it would result in a virtual repudiation of the Cultural Revolution as well as endangering their political future. In fact, Chiang Ching bitterly complained in mid-March 1968 that a wave of "rightist deviationism" had suddenly become the main danger to Communist China.

The radical leaders in the Maoist camp in Peking and many Maoist organizations (especially the Red Guards and other extremists) across the country, which had close connections with Chiang Ching and her Cultural Revolution Group, were disappointed about the fact that the long turmoil of the Cultural Revolution had not brought the sweeping revolutionary changes that it had seemed to promise. They were disenchanted with the faltering direction of the Cultural Revolution and with the governing Revolutionary Committees which, in many cases, gave the Maoists only subsidiary power under the domination of military generals and rehabilitated Party-government cadres. In their eyes, those rehabilitated bureaucrats were virtually indistinguishable from their old comrades who had been formerly purged as persons "walking the capitalist road." In the past two years, in the meantime, the loyal Maoist partisans in Peking and the provinces had acquired a stake in, and an emotional commitment to, continued ferment; and a rehabilitation of the officials previously "dragged out" and denounced as anti-Maoist "black gang of demons, freaks and ghosts" posed a political threat to them. Therefore, they were aspiring to recover the power they had enjoyed once, and clamoring for a "radical change."

A fresh directive by Mao and the Maoist press in the spring of 1968 approving "proletarian factionalism" served as the green light to the Maoist revolutionary left, especially the young Red Guards, to resume their disruptive factional activities after months of hesitation. Factional violence intensified and by June, 1968, approached the 1967 summer's levels. The most troubled areas were in Communist China's southern half, and the Maoist factional strife there degenerated into a form of provincial civil war, even surpassing the 1967 summer's levels.[21] Savage fighting between rival Maoist factions in southern China in the first half of 1968 reportedly cost the lives of more than 50,000 people on one side alone.[22]

Maoist "rebel" factions were bitterly divided into radical and moderate groups. (The radical groups supported Chiang Ching and her leftist policies, but the moderate groups supported Premier Chou En-lai's policy of order and stability.) As with most factions elsewhere in Communist China, their enmities were based less on ideology (both groups professed to be loyal to Chairman Mao and his ideology) than on matters of self-interest, i.e., power, authority, and influence.

A faint glimpse of the factional disorder and violence in South China in the summer of 1968 was visible as nearly a hundred corpses, plainly victims of violence, washed ashore in Hong Kong and nearby Macao. Factional fighting had spread to fifty-six cities, counties, and towns in Kwangsi in the summer of 1968, and both sides used modern weapons and ammunitions. Savage fighting, murder, arson, looting, and disruption as well as destruction of railroads from April to July, 1968, had left thousands of houses burned out, about 50,000 Red Guards killed, and Soviet military and economic supplies to North Vietnam waylaid.[23] In Kwangtung, for example, local people had raided trains bound for Hanoi to steal badly needed food and medicine. Arms shipments had also been looted by Red Guards and other Maoist "rebels" seeking weapons. Peking's urgent orders to stop fighting, restore rail traffic, and return all Hanoi-bound weapons were repeatedly ignored by the Red Guards. Thousands of refugees were known to have fled. Radical Maoist factions in South China and elsewhere had accused the army of not supporting them in factional quarrels with conservative Maoist groups.

In general, the army had not intervened in renewed factional strife, in keeping with a directive from Mao that prohibited it from interfering with or suppressing the activities of the Maoist revolutionary left. But in some areas of South China the ruling army command had repeatedly taken a tougher line towards the increasing clashes between rival Red Guard factions, and openly favored moderate (or conservative) factions against radical groups linked closely to Chiang Ching and her Cultural Revolution Group. As a result, some radical Red Guard factions lost out in bloody battles with more moderate factions who were backed by the moderate, law-and-order-minded local army commanders. These military officers were out of favor with the leftist leadership in Peking, but they may well have had the tacit support of the civilian moderates, headed by Premier Chou En-lai, and senior military leaders.

As a result of the renewed factional fighting across the country in the summer of 1968, heavy damage was inflicted on Communist China's industry, railways, ports, and other communication facilities. Speaking to a conference of transport workers in Peking in May, 1968, Premier Chou En-lai acknowledged that factional fighting and sabotage in a key railway junction in the southern Kwangsi border area had paralyzed even the movement of Soviet military and economic supplies to North Vietnam.[24]

In late July, 1968, Chairman Mao apparently decided to take steps to crack down on this fresh phase of turmoil. Moderate leaders in Peking apparently convinced Mao and his chief aide, Defense Minister Lin Piao, that to let the mounting factional strife go on would risk national disintegration, so the time had come to bring rampant Red Guard factional struggles to a halt. Whether in response to this pressure upon Mao or not, Mao himself apparently decided to turn his back on the Red Guards in the fall of 1968.

It is quite apparent that even Chairman Mao was disillusioned with the Red Guards, whom he once hailed as "forerunners" of his Cultural Revolution. According to reliable

Hong Kong sources of August, 1968, Mao Tse-tung personally summoned five Peking Red Guard representatives at three o'clock on the morning of July 28, 1968, and for the next five hours flayed them for their disunity and failure to measure up to his "revolutionary" standards.[25] These sources describe Mao as having broken down and wept as he told these senior Red Guard leaders that their unprincipled factional fighting was responsible for provoking the trend toward military (not "proletarian") rule in China. "You have let me down," he reportedly told them, "and, what is more, you have disappointed the workers, peasants, and soldiers of China."[26] After this session, Mao's favored Red Guards were suddenly vilified as disruptive "troublemakers" and decadent "intellectuals" and their putdown was in full swing.

On August 1, 1968 (Peking's Army Day), Chairman Mao perhaps reluctantly approved directives authorizing the army to suppress Maoist factional fighting and halt the leftist-extremists' militant struggle for power, with arms if necessary. Chairman Mao's approval of the growing political role of the army was contained in an editorial printed jointly in three major Maoist publications, *Jen-min Jih-pao*, *Hung Ch'i*, and *Chieh-fang-chün Pao*, to celebrate the forty-first anniversary of the founding of the Chinese People's Liberation Army. The editorial accorded the Army virtually a free hand to deal with disorderly Maoist "rebel" elements on the left and right, creating the impression that the Maoist leadership in Peking was prepared to repudiate the Red Guard's pioneering role and whatever merits they had had during the initial period of the Cultural Revolution.[27] The production of posters and publishing of papers by the Red Guards were put under army control. The army was instructed to normalize railway traffic where it had been disrupted in the spring and summer of 1968, particularly along the Vietnam supply route through Kwangsi, and to push through the formation of new Revolutionary Committees, irrespective of factional interests.[28]

The Army Day editorial described the Revolutionary Committees, now set up in most of Communist China's twenty-nine provinces as the country's "organs of power," to be obeyed by "all units." The army was directed to back all Revolutionary Committees, at all levels of administration, and to defend themselves from enemies on the right or "extreme left."

Closely related to the above measures was a directive from Chairman Mao proclaiming that the workers and peasants were the most reliable and honored revolutionary group and, together with the army, were "the main force," who should be given a predominant role in the Cultural Revolution and "in all fields of work."[29] (It is significant that this directive followed by one day the second anniversary of the political debut of the Red Guards in Peking—August 18.) In announcing this new policy, Mao made it clear that a special place of honor previously enjoyed by student Red Guards—who in the Maoist lexicon fall in the category of intellectuals—was at an end, and that they, along with more elderly intellectuals, must "reform" themselves and integrate with the workers and the peasants in a subordinate role.[30] The Maoist press warned that the leadership in Peking would "advise those university students who think they are superior and look down upon the worker-peasant masses not to do that any more." All Red Guards should take the workers as their teachers and accept their hegemony without reservation.

Another directive from Mao ordered the workers and soldiers in the cities and the peasants and the soldiers in the countryside to take over all educational institutions, suppress the factionalism, and rectify ideological errors of students and teachers.[31] Moderate military authorities in Peking and most of Communist China's provinces had not concealed their intention to exploit Mao's new directives to crack down on the riotous Red Guards and other Maoist radicals to the extent that the Cultural Revolution could be brought to an end in all but name. Reliable sources from Hong Kong indicated that the new directives from Mao had been carried out with brutal enthusiasm by army-worker-peasant elements giving vent to long-suppressed hatred for Red Guard excesses. (In this campaign, the workers and peasants virtually served as deputized agents of the army.) The youthful Red Guard organizations had been ordered to disband, and Red Guard leaders in major cities and provinces had been arrested along with thousands of their followers, with those found guilty of certain crimes being publicly executed. The Red Guards were sent back to classrooms for study under a reformed educational system initiated by Mao.[32] At the same time, hundreds of thousands of the Red Guards were shipped to rural areas or remote border regions to do years of penance (i.e., manual labor) in mines, factories, communes, and forestation projects.[33] According to Chinese Nationalist intelligence sources, Chinese Communist authorities in Peking, Shanghai, and other cities were canceling the food ration cards of students who evaded orders transferring them to work gangs in the countryside.[34] (In connection with this program, the Mao-Lin regime also moved vast numbers of urban dwellers to China's rural and remote border areas in one of the most massive compulsory migrations in history. According to Hong Kong estimates, at least 20 million people had been moved out of cities by early 1969.)[35] By December, 1968, at least 3,190,000 students of five major cities and twelve provinces had reportedly been "resettled" in the countryside.[36] In some provinces, villagers had beaten groups of Red Guards to death. In short, Communist China recently embarked on a new top-priority purge with strong anti-intellectual overtones.

In August, 1968, disciplinary platoons of soldiers, workers, and peasants, euphemistically called "Mao Tse-tung's Thought Propaganda Teams," began to take over universities, secondary schools, and other haunts of intellectuals to curb their tendency toward extreme leftism and lack of discipline.[37] (The precise role of these new teams was never clearly defined, but most of the teams seemed to be instruments of the provincial-level Revolutionary Committees controlled by the army.) They entered radio stations, hospitals, science and research centers, art and literature centers, publishing houses, stores, and other places in which Red Guard factions were fighting among themselves or resisting army control.

By and large, these and other measures against the Red Guards reflected a conservative or moderate trend that gradually took shape in late July, 1968, after attempts by Chiang Ching and her leftist colleagues in Peking in the spring of 1968 to regenerate the Cultural Revolution had ignited widespread violence, particularly in South China.

The moderate trend that developed in the latter part of 1968 was also reflected in the economic sector, where considerable effort was put into getting production back to normal after the serious decline in 1967 and the first half of 1968.

The trend toward moderation carried over into foreign affairs as well. The Chinese Communists worked to repair some of the diplomatic fences damaged during the Red Guard rampages of 1966 and 1967. Main emphasis was on restoring economic relations.

Communist China's policies toward the United States, the Soviet Union, and the Vietnam war remained as belligerent as ever, but generally cautious in approach.

By September 6, 1968, all of the provincial-level Revolutionary Committees had been formed throughout the country. (But the process of forming revolutionary committees at the sub-provincial level—in counties, cities, factories, schools, communes, and production brigades—continued throughout 1969 and 1970.) Of the twenty-nine provincial Revolutionary Committees, twenty-one were headed by military persons, and the remaining eight generally had powerful military vice-chairmen. The Red Guards and other Maoist radicals were either excluded or relegated to minor positions in the twenty-one provincial Revolutionary Committees ruled by the army. Within the central government, most of the state ministries were taken over by the military.[38]

By the time all of the country's twenty-nine provincial-level Revolutionary Committees were established in the fall of 1968, the majority of them were unwieldy bodies, with a dozen or more men of little experience and often with antagonistic factional backgrounds, except for the army officers, designed more to set local policy and to perform elemental government functions. (The provincial-level Revolution Committee is now divided into five departments: Administrative, Political, Security, Revolution and Production, and Civil Affairs.)[39] The violence and disruption of earlier periods of the Cultural Revolution no longer prevailed, but purges and power struggles continued in China's provinces as leftists, rightists, and moderates tried to outmaneuver one another despite Peking's appeals for unity. Almost every provincial Revolutionary Committee complained to one degree or another of the continuing opposition of "class enemies" who would not accept the power structure of the Revolutionary Committees. There were attacks from the right, the cadres of the old Party structure who once ruled the country, and the left, the radical elements who still stung from the exile of the Red Guards or from their exclusion from authority by the military. Strong differences between the military and civilians were also evident in a number of provinces.

Ironically, it was apparent that the army-controlled Revolutionary Committees in most of Communist China's twenty-nine provinces, despite their establishment in the name of the Cultural Revolution, were *de facto* regional military juntas— dedicated less to promoting Mao's ambitious ideological rectification campaign than to halting the widespread turmoil. Instead of infusing their committees with "new [Maoist] blood," many provincial military commanders in power were bringing back the old (purged or disgraced) Party and government bureaucrats familiar with government and administration. What was more important, these conservative or moderate military men were becoming a new vested interest—much like the vested interest of the Party apparatus destroyed by the Maoist revolutionary leftists some time ago. While loudly paying lip service to Maoism and the Cultural Revolution, they seemed reluctant to surrender their newly gained power to the theoretical central authority in Peking, which is armed neither with guns nor with economic control, but only with directives from Chairman Mao and the Thought of Mao Tse-tung.

At the end of 1968, by and large, the Chinese Communist regime, which once seemed to be a highly centralized monolith, was unraveling into a loose array of provincial power structures shaping policy directives from Peking to conform with local conditions and interests.[40] When Mao and his Proletarian Headquarters in Peking reluctantly assigned the mission of pacification to the local military commanders, they virtually abdicated their own authority—and formally endorsed the effective decentralization of power.

The Mao-Lin regime in Peking lost no time in expressing concern at the failure of some provincial authorities to implement directives of the central government. This concern was expressed in a joint editorial of January 1, 1969, in *Jen-min Jih-pao, Hung Ch'i,* and *Chieh-fang-chün Pao,* the capital's three major Maoist publications. The editorial called on the people of China to "rally closely around the Proletarian Headquarters" headed by Mao Tse-tung and Lin Piao. It said that those who did not implement the policies of the Proletarian Headquarters were disloyal to Chairman Mao. It added that they were, in essence, attempting to set up "bourgeois independent kingdoms and to spread the bourgeois reactionary theory of many centers." It also attacked those who did not implement central government policies "under the pretext of special circumstances and local conditions."

In January, 1969, however, Mao's Proletarian Headquarters in Peking appeared to be taking a temperate approach toward the maverick provinces, using, instead of threats, more gentle forms of persuasion. This perhaps was evidence that the central Maoist command in Peking was not in position to enforce its directives in some provinces.

As a result of the new moderate trend in the Cultural Revolution in the fall of 1968, Mao Tse-tung's wife, Chiang Ching, and her leftist leaders in Peking appeared to be losing authority. Since Chiang Ching herself is considered too close to her husband to be toppled, the moderate leaders in Peking, headed by Premier Chou En-lai and senior military officers, have since late 1968 been seeking to isolate and neutralize her by eliminating her most dynamic and radical partisans.

But, as far as was known on the basis of available evidence, the leftist leaders in Peking were not yet politically finished in early 1969, indicating that they would be expected to fight back again. There seemed to be a form of uneasy political stalemate in the Maoist command in Peking between moderate and radical elements, so neither of them was strong enough to come out as a clear and final winner.

In the 1968 National Day (October 1) celebration in Peking, Premier Chou En-lai said "Long live the Red Guards" in his speech and then announced a new policy that unspecified numbers of the youth must "go to the hilly areas and countryside and work in factories and rural areas."[41] While this policy was clearly meant to limit the Red Guards' unprincipled and wild political activity and power, a rearguard action was begun immediately by leftist leaders in Peking who had always encouraged and supported their disruptive activities. On the same day that Premier Chou spoke, Chiang Ching tepidly endorsed the ideological remolding of the youths, but said that Communist China must not forget that the Red Guards "have won great merits" and that they must be protected, apparently from reprisal.[42]

The Red Guard formations, placed near the rear of the parade in 1968, instead of at the head as in the past two National Day demonstrations, wore sashes of the color symbol of the workers—blue—as a tangible symbol of their ideological subjugation, but did not lose their militant appearance. Still wearing military-type uniforms, they waved tiny red booklets of *Quotations from Chairman Mao Tse-tung* and shouted slogans more loudly than others.

In early 1969, Peking launched a campaign to rebuild the entire Chinese Communist Party apparatus, shattered by the

Cultural Revolution, to replace the present inadequate and "temporary" organs of power at levels of Communist China. Party rebuilding itself was listed as one of the "major tasks" for 1969 by the Mao-Lin regime.[43]

But the Maoist camp seemed to be divided into two factions on the question of how the Party should be rebuilt.[44] Both sides seemed to agree on the necessity of reconstructing the Party in order to provide the country with a cohesive nation-wide political and administrative apparatus. However, they differed essentially on what role in a new organization should be given to the Red Guards and other Maoist revolutionary leftist groups.

The leftist faction in Peking apparently favored a wide-ranging expulsion of older Party members and the inclusion of a large number of young Maoist "activists" who had emerged during the Cultural Revolution, in order to infuse the Party with new blood.[45] In other words, Mao's leftist colleagues in Peking favored the admission of new dynamic Maoist leftists who were loyal to it. As they saw it, the elimination of the Red Guards and other pro-Mao "revolutionary rebel" groups from a new Party structure would undermine their power base throughout the country, leaving them "a kind of palace coterie depended solely on Mao's prestige and favor," as Stanley Karnow aptly puts. (But the odds did not seem to favor this leftist factional view, since the moderates, widely represented in the majority of the country's twenty-nine provincial-level Revolutionary Committees, had been cracking down on the unruly young Maoist "activists" since September, 1968.)

But the moderate faction in Peking probably favored the rehabilitation of large numbers of old Party officials who had been purged or denounced during the Cultural Revolution, and was evidently anxious to exclude the Red Guards and other Maoist "activists" from a renovated Party machine, or at least accord them only minimal recognition. These high-ranking moderates, mainly concerned with restoring peace and order to their country after almost three years of turmoil, were reluctant to refurnish the Party with the same elements responsible for the past turbulence.

Obviously, the solution of this important factional difference in Peking was the factor deciding how soon the Ninth Congress of the Chinese Communist Party could be held. Often postponed for various reasons, the Congress was about ten years overdue under the Party Constitution. (The 1956 Party Constitution stipulated that a National Party Congress was to be held every five years. The Eighth Party Congress was held in 1956.) The Ninth Party Congress would "legally" validate changes made during the Cultural Revolution, approve the formal investiture of the new Maoist leadership team in Peking, and set policy for Communist China's future.

The Enlarged Twelfth Plenum of the Eighth Central Committee of the Chinese Communist Party was held in Peking between October 11 and 31, 1968. As two leading Communist newspapers in Hong Kong conceded,[46] the Plenum was a "packed" session in which, to attain the majority for Chairman Mao, "revolutionary" outsiders (nonmembers) attended with full right. It dismissed Liu Shao-ch'i, the chief of state and former deputy chairman of the Party, from all his Party and government posts, although, it must be noted, the Central Committee of the Chinese Communist Party theoretically or "legally" does not have the authority to remove the chief of state, as his post is filled by the election of the National People's Congress. (The last National People's Congress was held in 1965.) The session ratified everything Chairman Mao and his Maoist colleagues had done during the Cultural Revolution, of which Mr. Liu had been the chief target.[47]

The Plenum also approved a draft text of a new Constitution for the Chinese Communist Party which was then circulated throughout China for discussion before the convocation of the forthcoming Ninth Party Congress.[48] The draft Party Constitution was believed to have been written by Mao Tse-tung himself or at least under his personal direction. It was an affirmation of the dominance of Maoism and of opposition to

Soviet-style "revisionism" and "neo-capitalism." Much of the draft was devoted to the glorification of the Thought of Mao Tse-tung, describing Mao as the political heir of Marx and Lenin. It made Chairman Mao's views and his sinicized formulations of Marxism and Leninism the official doctrine and gospel of the Chinese mainland. It also formally made Mao's handpicked heir, Defense Minister Lin Piao, as the Chairman's successor when Mao dies or is forced to step down by reason of health.

Finally, the Plenum decided that the Ninth Party Congress would be held "at an appropriate time," indicating that the Peking leadership was embarking on a new effort to set guidelines for stability, moderation, construction, and unity at the forthcoming Party Congress.

NOTES TO CHAPTER 3

1. See, for example, *Shanghai Wen Hui Pao*, October 15, 1967, and January 12, 1968.

2. *Jen-min Jih-pao*, September 17, 1967; *Chieh-fang chün Pao*, September 17, 1967; *New China News Agency*, October 10, 1967; and "Order Issued by CCP Central Committee, the State Council, Central Military Affairs Commission, and Central Cultural Revolution Group Forbidding Seizure of Arms, Equipment, and Other Military Supplies from the PLA," in *SCMP*, No. 4026, pp. 1–2.

3. *Ibid.* See also *Chieh-fang-chün Pao*, January 28, 1968.

4. *Chieh-fang-chün Pao*, October 20, 1967.

5. *Jen-min Jih-pao*, October 19 and 21, 1967; and *Chieh-fang-chün Pao*, January 28, 1968. The army was also assigned the main responsibility for promoting "revolutionary great alliances" in both schools and factories. *Chieh-fang-chün Pao*, September 17, 1967.

6. *Jen-min Jih-pao*, October 8, 9, 25, 1967; and November 26, 1967.

7. *Chieh-fang-chün Pao*, October 20, 1967; and *Jen-min Jih-pao*, October 21 and 25, 1967.

8. See *Current Scene*, June 1, 1968, pp. 1–37; October 18, 1968, pp. 1–28; and December 6, 1968, pp. 1–16. See also Winberg Chai, "The Reorganization of the Chinese Communist Party, 1966–68," *Asian Survey*, November 1968, pp. 901–910; and Richard Baum, "China: Year of the Mangoes," *Asian Survey*, January 1969, pp. 5–9.

9. *Ibid.*

10. *Ibid.*

11. *Ibid.*

12. See footnote 3 of this chapter.

13. *Shanghai Wen Hui Pao,* January 7 and 10, 1968; and *Chieh-fang-chün Pao,* January 10, 1968.

14. *The China Quarterly,* July–September 1968, p. 177. For Chiang Ching's personal biography see Hao-Jan Chu, "Mao's Wife—Chiang Ch'ing," *ibid.,* July–September, 1967, pp. 148–150; and *Current Scene,* January 6, 1969, pp. 1–12.

15. *Far Eastern Economic Review,* Hong Kong, July 18, 1969, p. 149.

16. *Canton Chungshan University Combat News,* No. 47, April 14, in the *Survey of the China Mainland Press,* No. 4173, May 8, 1968, p. 5.

17. *Shanghai Wen Hui Pao,* April 15, 1968; *Jen-min Jih-pao,* April 10, 1968; and May 16, 1968; *Hung Ch'i,* May 16, 1968; and *Chieh-fang-chün Pao,* May 16, 1968.

18. *Jen-min Jih-pao,* April 19 and 27, 1968. See also *New China News Agency,* June 6, 1968.

19. *Shanghai Wen Hui Pao,* June 6 and 7, 1968; and *Jen-min Jih-pao,* June 2, 1968; and *Chieh-fang-chün Pao,* June 2, 1968.

20. *Shanghai Wen Hui Pao,* June 9, 1968.

21. See *The New York Times,* June 20, 1968, p. 5; July 14, 1968, pp. 1–5; and *The Washington Post,* June 30, 1968, pp. 1, 20; and July 17, 1968, p. 12.

22. *The New York Times,* September 22, 1968, p. 11.

23. *New China News Agency,* May 26, 1968; *Shanghai Radio,* June 3, 1968; and "Notice of CCP Central Committee, State Council, Military Commission of Central Committee and Central Cultural Revolution Group, dated July 1968," *Canton Middle School Red Guards,* No. 8, late-July 1968, translated in the *Survey of Chinese Mainland Press,* No. 4232, August 6, 1968, pp. 1–13. See also *The New York Times,* June 28, 1968, p. 1; July 10, 1968, pp. 1, 8; and *The Washington Post,* July 12, 1968, pp. 1, 16; July 13, 1968, pp. 1, 14.

24. *Ibid.*

25. Stanley Karnow's reports in *The Washington Post,* August 14, 1968, p. 20; August 28, 1968, p. 12; Tillman Durdin's report in *The New York Times,* September 1, 1968, p. 10. See also *Far Eastern Economic Review,* Hong Kong, August 29, 1968, pp. 377–378.

26. *Ibid.*

27. See also *Jen-min Jih-pao,* August 18, 1968.

28. *Jen-min Jih-pao,* August 5, 1968; and August 13, 1968; *Chieh-fang-chün Pao,* August 5, 1968; and August 13, 1968.

29. *Jen-min Jih-pao,* August 18, 1968; September 25, 1968; November 25, 1968; *Chieh-fang-chün Pao,* September 25, 1968; and November 25, 1968; Yao Wen-yuan, "The Working Class Must Exercise Leadership in Everything," *Hung Ch'i,* August 15, 1968; and *Hung Ch'i,* November 25, 1968.

30. *Ibid.*

31. *Jen-min Jih-pao,* September 15, 1968; and November 10, 1968.

32. For Chairman Mao's new educational policy see Chapter 5 of this book.

33. *Jen-min Jih-pao,* October 5, 1968; *Peking Radio,* October 4, 1968; and *New China News Agency,* November 2 and 19, 1968.

34. *The* (Baltimore) *Sun,* December 30, 1968, p. 8.

35. See *What's Happening on the Chinese Mainland,* Taipei, Republic of China, March 9, 1969, p. 1.

36. *Ibid.*

37. *Peking Review,* August 9, 1968, pp. 5–6.

38. See *What's Happening on the Chinese Mainland,* February 8, 1970, pp. 1–2.

39. The Editor, "The Revolutionary Committee and the Party in the Aftermath of the Cultural Revolution," *Current Scene,* April 15, 1970, p. 5.

40. See, for example, *Jen-min Jih-pao,* August 13, 1968; and *Shanghai Wen Hui Pao,* August 5, 1968; and August 7, 1968.

41. *Peking Review,* October 4, 1968, pp. 14–15.

42. *The New York Times,* October 2, 1968, pp. 1, 3.

43. *Jen-min Jih-pao,* January 1, 1969.

44. Stanley Karnow's report in *The Washington Post,* October 15, 1968, p. 16. See also *The New York Times,* October 14, 1968, p. 2.

45. *Jen-min Jih-pao,* October 22, 1968; *Shanghai Wen Hui Pao,* October 5, 14, 15 and 16, 1968; and *The China Quarterly,* January–March 1968, pp. 150–152.

46. *Shanghai Wen Hui Pao,* November 24, 1968; and *Ta Kung Pao,* December 3, 1970.

47. *Peking Review,* Supplement, November 1, 1968, pp. v–viii.

48. For the full text of the draft of the proposed constitution of the Chinese Communist Party see *The New York Times,* January 8, 1969, p. 6; and *The China Quarterly,* January–March 1969, pp. 169–174.

CHAPTER 4

The Ninth Party Congress
and After

THE LONG-DELAYED Ninth National Congress of the Chinese
Communist Party was convened in Peking on April 1, 1969,
and lasted until April 24, 1969. This Party Congress was the
ninth since the Chinese Communist Party was founded in
Shanghai in 1921, only the third in the last forty years and the
second since Mao and his Communist colleagues assumed control of the mainland in 1949.

The National Congress of the Chinese Communist Party, as
of Communist parties in general, is in theory the highest leading body in the Party's organizational structure. It elects the
Party's Central Committee, which sets Party policy during the
period between congresses and in turn selects the Politburo,
the ruling leadership group. Party congresses also set the gen
eral direction of domestic and foreign policies and shed light on
existing power relationships.

The Ninth Party Congress was expected to approve a new
Party charter, as the last two meetings adopted new Party Constitution. The main objective of the present Congress was to
end formally the most disruptive stage of Mao's Cultural
Revolution (that is to say, to affirm the illegality of the Maoist
takeover of the Party during the Cultural Revolution) and set
China on the path back to stability through the reconstruction
of its shattered Communist political apparatus.

The Mao-Lin regime did not divulge the exact location of the meeting, but it was probably held in Peking's Chungnanhai district, an enclave reserved for high Party and government officials. In contrast to the previous Congresses, there were no foreign guests.

It was apparent that, on the eve of the Ninth Party Congress, Mao and his radical partisans were using the March, 1969, armed border clashes on the Ussuri River and the Soviet military threat on their borders to secure greater loyalty to the Maoist line.

The Peking announcement, a press communiqué of the Congress Secretariat, said that the 1,512 delegates to the Ninth Party Congress included "advanced elements of the Communist Party who emerged in the Great Proletarian Cultural Revolution," representatives of Party members in factories and farms, and student Red Guards who were attending a Party Congress "for the first time."[1] It also said that these delegates were elected "in accordance with the decision" made by Peking leaders last fall as well as through "full democratic consultation by Party organizations at various levels and after extensively seeking the opinion of the broad mass."[2] This probably meant that many of the delegates were hand-picked by the provincial-level Revolutionary Committees, in contravention of the 1956 Party Constitution which was still technically in effect. According to the 1956 party charter, delegates to Party Congresses were supposed to be elected by provincial and city Party committees. It was unlikely that such legal procedures were followed for the Ninth Party Congress, especially since many of those provincial and municipal committees had been virtually disbanded. In late 1968, in fact, the Maoists rejected the constitutional legality of election. "Blind faith in elections is conservative thinking," said the October 15, 1968 issue of *Hung Ch'i*. In short, the Maoist command in Peking "produced" rather than "elected" the delegates; but it had to compromise, and "consultations" plus "elections" were used. (This procedure undoubtedly benefited the military representatives in power in most of the country's twenty-nine provinces.)

All of the forces that had been tugging and hauling in different directions during the past three-year course of the Cultural Revolution were represented in the list of the 1,512 delegates to the Ninth Party Congress. The Congress was a meeting hatched by compromise—that is to say, a coalition of "leftists" and "moderates," with the army constituting a large percentage of the delegates (or exercising considerable influence).

Mao opened the Ninth Party Congress with a short but "most important" speech, but the Peking announcement did not disclose the text. After Mao had declared the Congress opened, a Presidium was elected as one of the first acts of the Party Congress. Mao was unanimously elected Chairman, Lin Piao Vice-Chairman, and Chou En-lai Secretary-General of the Presidium Secretariat. Elected to the Presidium were 176 members, which represented an uneasy coalition of rival leftist and moderate elements with a heavy admixture of law-and-order-oriented military men.[3]

Along with Mao and Lin Piao, eight of the top fourteen members of the Presidium were unmistakably Mao's ardent supporters. Of the 176 members of the Presidium, about fifty (thirty per cent) were probably Maoist "proletarian revolutionaries"—workers, peasants, a very few Red Guards, and representatives of other pro-Mao mass organizations. The appearance on the list of these Maoist radicals could be regarded as evidence that Mao's desire for "fresh blood" in the Party was partially satisfied. But this Maoist representation was counterbalanced by moderate-minded delegates mostly from the provinces, who, as a whole, constituted about fifty-five to sixty per cent of the Presidium list. At least sixty-five delegates (about thirty-six per cent) of the Presidium were readily identifiable army officers, most of whom, as chairmen or vice-chairmen of the Revolutionary Committees in the majority of China's twenty-nine provinces, had been trying to curb the excesses of the Cultural Revolution. The large number of military delegates to the Ninth Party Congress and its Presidium was testimony to the army's emergence as the single most powerful and cohesive force in the Cultural Revolution. The rest of the Presidium delegates (about forty-five to fifty) included seasoned or old-line Party bureaucrats, who survived Mao's wild Cultural Revolution, and civilian officials from government, scientific, and cultural circles.

The Ninth Party Congress had three important items on the agenda—(1) the presentation of a political report on the domestic and international situation by Defense Minister Lin Piao; (2) the adoption of a draft new Party Constitution to replace the old one of 1956; and (3) the election of a new Central Committee of the Chinese Communist Party.

The Congress proceeded with the first item on the agenda. At the opening session of April 1, Lin Piao, Mao's chosen heir, gave his report, which summed up the genesis, development, and future perspective of the Cultural Revolution.[4] By any objective standards, Lin's 24,000-word report was a harsh, tough, belligerent, and chest-thumping speech. Yet it contained no major surprises and advocated no radical policy shifts. It was stronger on generalities than on specifics, and dealt more with the past than with the future. Radical in its loyal presentation of revolutionary and idealistic Maoism, it was cautious when it left the realm of theory. Overall, it was a document of compromise both for Chinese domestic and foreign policies.

Lin Piao's speech dealing with the domestic affairs of China can be broken down into the following important points:

(1)   A great (not final or total) victory of the Cultural Revolution against China's "revisionist" enemies led by Liu Shao-ch'i.
(2)   Continuation of Mao's "permanent revolution" (i. e., uninterrupted "class struggle") within China, but in a more orderly fashion, until the total victory of the Maoist-type Communist revolution at home and abroad is attained.

(3) Proclamation of Mao Tse-tung's Thought, in equal status with Marxism-Leninism, as the sole orthodox ideology and guide to all the actions of the people of China.

(4) Primacy of the army in the affairs of Communist China: The army is "the mighty pillar of the dictatorship of the proletariat" and the "main component of the state."

(5) Leniency toward and rehabilitation of the purged or disgraced Party cadres in Mao's Cultural Revolution.

Nothing was said in Lin's report about another Great Leap Forward experiment which some Maoist radicals had advocated during the past three years.[5] This implied that there would be no repetition of the disastrous economic and social practices that marked Mao's Great Leap Forward campaign of 1958. Politics was to be elevated as the "lifeblood" of the country, said Lin. But then he warned that he was not trying "to replace production by revolution but to use revolution to command production." Lin seemed to imply that sound economic policies would take precedence over revolutionary ideals.

Nor was anything mentioned in Lin's report on such specific agricultural policies as abolishing peasants' private plots and the private market place, as some radical Maoists had proposed. Nothing was said about a massive decentralization of the economy, health, or education.

Defense Minister Lin Piao appeared to be charting a course between excessive ideological zeal and all-pervasive pragmatism. His policies, if implemented, would maintain China's revolutionary fervor while pursuing practical ends. Such a middle-of-the-road course seemed designed to appease Peking's radical factions, which put ideology first, while satisfying moderates, who stress realistic political and economic approaches.

By and large, the guidelines Lin set down in his report for future political and economic policies seemed to suggest that the Peking leadership, while employing militant Maoist rhetoric, was seeking to restore stability and unity following

China's most turbulent period since the Communists took power two decades ago.

Lin Piao's speech dealing with international relations was nothing but a restatement of the Maoist hard-line view of world affairs. Nothing came out of his speech to indicate any early change from the isolationist, xenophobic attitudes shown during the height of the Cultural Revolution. The foreign policy section of Mr. Lin's speech included the following points:

(1) Peking's continuing militant stance toward its two great enemies, "United States imperialism" and "Soviet revisionism," and the importance of full preparations for a full-scale nuclear war with them.

(2) Continued cooperation with other Communist states and "peaceful coexistence" with other non-Communist ones.

(3) Reaffirmation of a Maoist theory that war between capitalism and Communism is inevitable unless forestalled by Communist revolution.

(4) A complete restatement of Chinese Communist determination to support and encourage all "revolutionary struggles" and "wars of national liberation" throughout the underdeveloped world.[6]

(5) A clarion call for a united front of nations and peoples subject to "bullying" by the United States and the Soviet Union, to resist Soviet and American efforts to divide up the world and their common enemies.

(6) Reiteration of Peking's determination to liberate China's "sacred territory" of Taiwan.

(7) Condemnation of the Soviet occupation of Czechoslovakia, the Brezhnev Doctrine, and Moscow's March, 1969, border provocations in the Ussuri River.

After Lin's address, the 1,512 delegates split up into small working groups to discuss Lin's report and the draft of the revised Constitution of the Chinese Communist Party.

On April 14, 1969, the Ninth Party Congress unanimously approved Lin Piao's report along with a new Party Constitution.[7]

The new Party Constitution of 1969 differed only in minor phrases and languages from the draft that was produced at a plenary session of the Party Central Committee in October, 1968, and circulated throughout the country after that. In contrast to the old 1956 Party Constitution which contained nine chapters and sixty articles, the new Constitution was compact, comprising six chapters and twelve articles.[8] More important, it was a loose and ambiguous document. The essential ambiguity of the new charter seemed to suggest that rival factions inside the Peking leadership, while all paying homage to Maoism and the personality cult of Mao Tse-tung, had not resolved the differences that had divided them during the course of the Cultural Revolution. It was also possible that its ambiguity was deliberately contrived by the moderates now ruling the country's twenty-nine provinces, to assure themselves of maximum flexibility to shape the reconstructed Party to fit their own interests.

The main characteristics of the new Party Constitution of 1969 were as follows: (1) the elevation of Mao Tse-tung to the same exalted philosophical rank as Marx and Lenin, calling his ideology "Marxism-Leninism-Mao Tse-tung Thought," and the declaration of Maoism as the basic law of the land; (2) the enthronement of Lin Piao as Chairman Mao's successor after the latter's retirement or death; (3) a reaffirmation of Mao's "permanent revolution under the dictatorship of the proletariat"; (4) unequivocal hostility against the Soviet Union and its "revisionist" policies at home and abroad; (5) continuing opposition to the United States and the Soviet Union in foreign affairs; (6) the simplification of the Party machinery; (7) the selection of leading Party officials through "democratic consultation" and election; (8) the admission of new members into the Party by recommendation rather than election and without serving a probationary period; and (9) a provision authorizing Party members to dissent from commands of lower-level Party bodies and take complaints directly to the Central Committee or even right up to Chairman Mao. (Point 8 was probably designed to permit the moderate army commanders and veteran Party officials now controlling most of the provinces to reconstruct local Party organizations with their own partisans. Point

9 could be used by Maoist radicals in Peking to prevent any control of local Party units by anti-Maoists.)

On April 24, 1969, the Ninth Party Congress concluded its meeting with the naming of a Central Committee of 170 full and 109 alternate members.[9] (*See Appendix I.*) (The Central Committee is supposed to act for the Congress, when the latter is not in session.) Only fifty-two members of the previous Eighth Central Committee were reelected, indicating that no less than two-thirds of the old 196-man (regular and alternate) Central Committee had vanished during the Cultural Revolution.

The largest in the Party history, the list of the 279 regular and alternate members of the Ninth Central Committee roughly represented a careful balance of rival political forces that emerged during the Cultural Revolution, and demonstrated the vastly increased political power of the military. Mao Tse-tung was re-elected as Chairman and Lin Piao was named Vice-Chairman. The new members of the Committee were listed, in a departure from the usual procedure, in the order of the number of strokes of the surname (the equivalent in Chinese to alphabetical order) with the exception of Mao and Lin Piao. (On May 20, 1969, the Peking announcement officially ranked Premier Chou En-lai third among Communist China's leaders, directly under Mao and Lin, for the first time since the Ninth Party Congress ended on April 24, 1969.)[10]

New blood was drawn from the Red Guards and other radical Maoist elements to give the new Central Committee the "proletarian" flavor, and confirmed Maoist radicals, once associated with the leftist excesses of the Cultural Revolution in 1966, 1967, and 1968, constituted about twenty-five per cent of the total members of the Committee. But these Maoist true believers were counterbalanced by pragmatic-minded civil officials and the army. (A few people who had been severely denounced by the Red Guards made a surprising comeback and were elected to the Central Committee. They included "General" Wang En-mao, former political and military boss of Sinkiang Province, and Yo Chiu-li, Minister of Petroleum.)

Roughly twenty-eight per cent of the total membership of the Committee were civilian Party and government figures, who included state ministers and officials of the central government, former provincial governors and deputy governors, members of former provincial Party secretariats, ambassadors and mayors. Total military representation on the Committee was about forty-one per cent, thereby constituting the largest single bloc in the Ninth Central Committee.[11] The majority of these military representatives, who were divided between line and political officers in roughly equal number, held both important military and leading Revolutionary Committee posts in the provinces. These officers were largely pragmatic military men, who had also demonstrated their disdain for radical Maoist revolutionary activities. (The military delegates from the Ministry of Defense and military headquarters in Peking constituted about twelve per cent of the total Committee membership.) All twenty-nine chairmen of provincial-level Revolutionary Committees, the great majority of whom were military officers, were elected to the new Central Committee, twenty-five of them as regular members. About 120 leading members of the country's twenty-nine provincial Revolutionary Committees became regular or alternate members of the Committee: of these about seventy were military men. One major characteristic of the composition of the Ninth Central Committee was a significant decentralization of political power.

The Politburo of the Chinese Communist Party and its standing committee were elected by the first plenary session of the Ninth Central Committee held on April 28, 1969.[12] (The five members of the new Politburo are concurrently members of the Politburo's Standing Committee. This five-man Standing Committee is empowered to make decisions when the Central Committee or the Politburo is not in session, which is most of the time.) The Peking announcement was silent about whether or when a new Party Secretariat to replace the purged one would be established to administer the new Party apparatus.

The names of the Party Politburo and its powerful Standing Committee were as follows:

The Party's Politburo

(CODE: CR—certified radical; QR—questionable radical; M—moderate; N—neutral or moderator between rival factions; O—old Politburo member; F—freshman or new Politburo member; @—attacked by the Red Guards in the past.)

Regulars:

1) Mao Tse-tung (CR/O) —Chairman of the Central Committee of the Chinese Communist Party

2) Lin Piao (CR/O) —Vice-Chairman of the Central Committee of the Chinese Communist Party

(The following are in the order of the number of strokes of the surnames.)

3) Yeh Chun (Mme. Lin Piao) (CR/F) —Member of the Cultural Revolution Group in the Army; Head of Lin Piao's office

4) Yeh Chien-ying (M/O/@) —Ex-Marshal; Member of the Party's Military Affairs Committee

5) Liu Po-cheng (M/O/@) —Ex-Marshal

6) Chiang Ching (Mme. Mao) (CR/F) —Deputy Director of the Party's Cultural Revolution Group; a "Cultural Adviser" to the Army

7) Chu Teh (M/O/@) —Ex-Marshal (the father of the Chinese People's Liberation Army)

8) Hsu Shih-yu (M/F/@) —A Vice Minister of the National Defense; Commander of the Nanking Military Region

9) Chen Po-ta (CR/F) (now in disgrace?) —Mao's ghostwriter; Peking's ideologue; Chairman of the Cultural Revolution Group

10) Chen Hsi-lien (M/F/@) —Commander of the Shenyang Military Region

11) Li Hsien-nien (M/O/@) —A Deputy Premier; Minister of Finance (Chou En-lai's protégé)

12) Li Tso-peng (QR/F) —First Political Commissar of the Navy; Member of the National Defense Council (Lin's protegé)

13) Wu Fa-hsien (M/F) —Air Force Commander

14) Chang Chun-chiao (CR/F) —Chairman of the Shanghai Municipal Revolutionary Committee

15) Chiu Hui-tso (QR/F) —Director of the General Rear Service Department of the Chinese People's Liberation Army (Lin Piao's protegé)

16) Chou En-lai (M/O) —Prime Minister; Secretary-General of the Presidium of the Ninth Party Congress

17) Yao Wen-yuan (CR/F) —Member of the Cultural Revolution Group, a leading member of the Shanghai Municipal Revolutionary Committee (reputed to be Mao Tse-tung's son-in-law)

18) Kang Sheng (CR/O) —In charge of Peking's secret police and intelligence apparatus

19) Huang Yung-sheng (M/F/@) —Chief of the Army's General Staff

20) Tung Pi-wu (M/O) —A Deputy Chief of State

21) Hsieh Fu-chih (CR/F) —Minister of Public Security; Chairman of the Peking Municipal Revolutionary Committee

Alternates

1) Chi Teng-kuei (CR/F) —Deputy Chairman of the Honan Revolutionary Committee

2) Li Hsueh-fang (M/O/@) (now in disgrace) —Former Chairman of the Hopeh Provincial Revolutionary Committee (used to be Teng Hsiao-p'ing's protegé but now Chou En-lai's protegé)

3) Li Teh-sheng (QR/F) —Chairman of the Anhwei Provincial Revolutionary Committee; Military Commander of the Anhwei Military District; Director of the General Political Department of the PLA

The Party's Politboro (Continued)

4) Wang Tung-hsing (CR/F)

    —Mao Tse-tung's old bodyguard; Deputy Minister of Public Se-curity

The Politburo's Standing Committee

(The following are in the order of the number of strokes of the surnames.)

1) Mao Tse-tung (old member)
2) Lin Piao (old member)

3) Chen Po-ta (new member)
    (now in disgrace)
4) Chou En-lai (old member)
5) Kang Sheng (new member)

As seen above, the official list of the new members of the Party's Politburo and its Standing Committee was painstakingly careful to list only Mao and Lin in order of precedence. After that, the other members of the two leading Party organizations were listed in the Chinese equivalent of alphabetical order. This device seemed a deliberate way of exalting the special status of Chairman Mao and Vice Chairman Lin, or of trying to make sure that no one could challenge Lin as Mao's successor.

Only ten of the old revised twenty-six-man Party Politburo[13] were reelected. Five old Politburo members were not reelected, but retained on the Ninth Central Committee. They were Chen Yi, ex-Marshal and Foreign Minister; Li Fu-chun, Chairman of the State Planning Commission; Chen Yun, an economic planner who had been largely inactive lately; Nieh Jen-cheng, a military man who heads Communist China's nuclear weapons development; and Hsu Hsiang-chen, ex-Marshal and member of the Party's Military Affairs Committee. (All of these five were considered to be moderates, and some of them were severely denounced by the Red Guards during the height of the Cultural Revolution.) The rest of the old Politburo members were purged.

Like the membership of the Central Committee, the list of the new twenty-five regular and alternate members of the Politburo seemed to indicate a compromise leadership coalition between radical and moderate elements in Peking's top Party hierarchy. The surest sign of compromise, one that must have been particularly painful and difficult for such certified Maoist radicals as Chiang Ching to accept, was the inclusion into the Politburo of leaders severely attacked by the Red Guards during the Cultural Revolution. No such balance, however, existed in the small but all-powerful five-man Standing Committee of the Politburo, which was weighted overwhelmingly in favor of radical Maoists.

The membership of the new Politburo was heavily weighted in favor of central officials, especially members of Mao's Proletarian Headquarters. Quite clearly, the Politburo was dominated by confirmed Maoist radicals, but the military also gained strong representation. The election of the new Politburo tended to diminish the already badly shattered ranks of experienced, able and moderate government administrators in China. With government administrators and technocrats reduced to their lowest level of power in the twenty-two-year history of the Chinese People's Republic, military men moved up to higher ranks to replace them.

By and large, what emerged from the power structure of the Ninth Party Congress was that the influence, or at least the comparative visibility, of the Maoist radicals increased as they went up the power pyramid. The strong representation of the military as a group in the Central Committee may mean little in terms of actual decision-making, since the Central Committee usually meets twice a year and, thus, can be easily bypassed by the Politburo and its Standing Committee, as it has often been the case in the past, when crucial decisions are made. (The Politburo and its Standing Committee operate on a full-time basis.) But Chairman Mao and his radical followers in Peking must certainly realize that it is the members of the Central Committee, and primarily the military officers now ruling the provinces, who have to implement these decisions. Since the provinces are today stronger vis-à-vis Peking than they were in the pre-Cultural Revolution period, intense bargaining between the center and the provinces over some important policy issues would inevitably have to take place as an essential ingredient of the new Chinese political process.

One interesting phenomenon occurring during the Ninth Party Congress was the emergence of the wives of five Chinese Communist leaders as powerful or important political personalities in the Peking hierarchy.[14] They were:

1) Chiang Ching (Mme. Mao Tse-tung)—58 years old—member of the Politburo
2) Yeh Chun (Mme. Lin Piao)—47 years old—member of the Politburo

3) Tsai Yi-ou (Mme. Kang Sheng)—around the early 60s
—member of the Central Committee
4) Teng Ying-chao (Mme. Chou En-lai)—68 years old—
member of the Central Committee
5) Tsai Chang (Mme. Li Fu-chun)—71 years old—member of the Central Committee

As indicated above, these women are the wives of China's three top-ranking Communists, Chairman Mao, Vice-Chairman Lin Piao, and Premier Chou En-lai, and of two other senior political figures, Kang Sheng and Li Fu-chun.

Chiang Ching, Yeh Chun, and Tsai Yi-ou have risen to political prominence only since the Cultural Revolution. A close personal and political friendship seems to have developed among these three women concurrently with the political alliance forged among their husbands. Chiang Ching is by far the most powerful woman in China, soaring within three years from total obscurity to a seat in the Party Politburo. She has often exercised authority second only to her husband in the past three years. Interestingly enough, the deification of Chairman Mao has been matched by the spectacular rise of his wife to a position of powerful influence. Yeh Chun and Tsai Yi-ou, who are all but colorless individuals by all accounts, have also risen from complete obscurity to the seats in the Politburo and the Central Committee, respectively.

Teng Ying-chao (Mme. Chou En-lai) and Tsai Chang (Mme. Li Fu-chun) were two of Communist China's most prominent women long before Chiang Ching emerged as a major political personality. They have long been veteran revolutionaries and high-ranking Party officials in their own right. They became revolutionary Communist activists while they were young students, spent their formative years in Paris, where they married their husbands and helped to found the French chapter of the Chinese Communist Party, and joined in the celebrated Long March of 1934-35. Both were also members of the Party's Central Committee before the Cultural Revolution started.[15] They do not appear to be particularly close to Chiang Ching personally. During the past five-year Cultural Revolution, therefore, they have tactfully remained withdrawn from the public eye, as if not wanting to compete with, or give offense to, Mme. Mao, the sharp-tongued former second-rate movie actress in Shanghai, who called Mme. Liu Shao-ch'i an American spy and a prostitute.

All in all, the Ninth Party Congress was willing to give Chairman Mao all the glory he and his radical partisans had sought, but seemed to be holding back and tactically cautious when the moment came to implement his militant version of Communism. That is to say, the meeting was calm, businesslike, and, more important, was far from being the rubber-stamp one for which Mao and Lin presumably hoped. There was enough evidence to suggest that the Ninth Party Congress was embroiled in dissension and serious policy disputes, so it had to go through long and difficult labor pains giving birth to the new upper echelons of the Chinese Communist Party as well as its future policy guidelines.

Firstly, the Ninth Party Congress was shrouded in unprecedent and total secrecy for nearly four weeks, and the Chinese Communist press and radio had maintained a total silence about the proceedings for two weeks. Foreign guests, even the Party delegates from Albania, Peking's staunchest ally in the Communist world, were not invited to attend the meeting. (Normally, Communist Party Congresses in China as well as other parts of the Communist world attract a large number of representatives from allied parties.) Peking probably did not want to have outside witnesses to whatever deliberations were taking place at the Ninth Party Congress.

Secondly, the draft Party Constitution was amended and Lin Piao's report was modified, unusual steps in Communist Congresses. The communiqué issued by the Secretariat of the Ninth Party Congress Presidium on April 14, 1969, said that the charter was adopted after the delegates "conscientiously discussed" it, "chapter by chapter and article by article."[16] (Some delegates were reported to have questioned why Defense Minister

Lin had to be named specifically in the Constitution, a step never having taken place. They were also believed to have asked what would happen to the succession problem if Lin died before Chairman Mao.)[17] It also stated that the Congress delegates "discussed again and again" Lin's report "paragraph by paragraph and sentence by sentence," making "many good proposals" for additions and revisions.[18] Even after the Lin report was adopted by the Congress, the communiqué said that the Secretariat was entrusted with making "modifications in wording" before it was published.[19] (According to the past precedents in the twenty-two-year history of the Chinese People's Republic, leading political leaders have not had their speeches corrected. In this case, the modifications probably were more significant, for Defense Minister Lin was speaking as Chairman Mao's designated successor.)

Thirdly, the Congress spent an extraordinary ten days to elect a new Central Committee. In addition, the Committee was enlarged by about a hundred seats to comprise 279 members, apparently to accommodate the assorted factions and individuals competing for power and influence.

Moreover, the fact that the membership lists of the Central Committee, the Politburo, and its Standing Committee were published in the Chinese equivalent of alphabetical order was a further hint that internal factional squabbling prevented the establishment of an acceptable ranking arrangement.

Fourthly, the Congress did little to clarify what economic, agricultural, and social programs Communist China would follow in the future and, while it was fairly militant in foreign policy, it was also fairly ambiguous. The absence of specific outlines for the future may have reflected the continued rivalries and differences of view between the many factions that emerged during the Cultural Revolution.

Fifthly, another hint that the Ninth Party Congress was beset by internecine troubles was given by Peking's repeated and almost desperate appeals for unity since the Congress convened on April 1, 1969. The Congress communiqué underlined the need for "unity in thinking, policy, plan, command, and action" based on Maoism.[20]

One remarkable achievement of the Ninth Party Congress was to formalize the renovation of the Chinese Communist Party as the "core of political power" in Communist China after three years of the turbulent Cultural Revolution, along with the adoption of the new Party Constitution. In other words, the high-level decision-making organs of the Chinese Communist Party—the Central Committee, the Politburo, and the Politburo's Standing Committee—were back in working order in 1969. The reorganization of the government apparatus (the State Council) virtually destroyed by the Cultural Revolution was to follow the rebuilding of the Party.

But this achievement was largely superficial. What the Ninth Party Congress had achieved was the rebuilding of the Party at the top level only. Accordingly, a massive amount of work remained to be done in reconstructing the Party apparatus at intermediate and basic levels of the society.

Even in the high echelons of the Party, many important organs, such as the Party Secretariat, the Party Control Commission, and the Central Committee's important subordinate bodies, had ceased functioning or had been impaired by the Cultural Revolution, and serious effort was needed if they were to be rebuilt.

In the government, over which the Party exercises control, the effect of Mao's Cultural Revolution had been devastating. After the purge of Liu Shao-ch'i, Mao's principal "revisionist" opponent, Communist China was in the peculiar position of not having an official head of state at the time of the Ninth Party Congress. Much had yet to be done in reorganizing the government apparatus before it would function normally.

In contrast to Mao's dream of infusing a newly renovated Party entirely with "fresh revolutionary blood" to make it his loyal tool, what had emerged from the Ninth Party Congress was a new kind of bureaucracy based on nominal coalition between moderates and radical Maoists. This uneasy coalition between rival factions and the accompanying struggles for power and influence within the superficially renovated Party apparatus were likely to impede rather than speed up the process of rebuilding the demolished Party in some effective form. The leadership in Peking and the Revolutionary Committees in China's twenty-nine provinces continued to be too faction-ridden to make the task of Party rebuilding easy.

The large military representation in the top level organs of the renovated Chinese Communist Party added to Chairman Mao's difficulties in rebuilding the Party and putting it once more, as he says, "in control of the gun." Indications were that the army commanders ruling the majority of the country's twenty-nine provinces would never really like to hand the great power put into their hands during the Cultural Revolution back to a reconstructed Communist Party. Therefore, Chairman Mao's greatest test right after the Ninth Party Congress was whether he could reassert really effective control in the provinces by reducing the army's current predominant power.

After the Ninth Party Congress, it appeared that the provincial-level Revolutionary Committees run mostly by moderate military officers would become the core of a newly renovated Party apparatus, indicating the army's key role in Communist China's provincial power structure.

By and large, the Ninth Party Congress implicitly brought a formal end to the contrived disruption of the Cultural Revolution and set the stage for an attempt to impose law and order, revitalize the economy, and arrive at (not clearly defined) domestic and foreign policies which the factions and individuals contending for power and influence would accept.

As soon as the Ninth Party Congress was over, a major effort was made by the Mao-Lin regime to heal wounds inflicted in the course of the Cultural Revolution. It began to launch a unity drive aimed at friends of erstwhile "revisionist" opponents denounced previously as "anti-Party, anti-Socialist" elements. A special effort was directed at unifying the armed forces behind the Mao-Lin leadership. For example, in mid-

May, 1969, Chairman Mao and Vice-Chairman Lin held a reception for 10,000 military representatives in Peking, at which three former "Marshals" of the Chinese People's Liberation Army, who had been dropped from the Party Politburo but kept on the Ninth Central Committee, were identified as vice-chairmen of the Central Committee's powerful Military Affairs Committee.[21] The emergence of these three men, Chen Yi, Hsu Hsiang-chien, and Nieh Jung-chen, in positions of significant military influence, despite their recent political downgrading, was undoubtedly Peking's bid to rally behind the leadership of Chairman Mao these well-known, high-ranking military officers and their followers in the army. (It was also at this reception that Premier Chou En-lai was officially confirmed as Communist China's No. 3 leader for the first time since the Ninth Party Congress ended on April 24, 1969.)[22]

Throughout the country, provincial newspapers have since April, 1969, been carrying editorials with a unity theme. The editorials appear to be directed at dissident factions (mostly pro-Mao leftist factions like Red Guard organizations) that do not favor making peace with former enemies.

Though retaining the heady Maoist rhetoric, the post-Ninth Party Congress Communist China makes it clear that the Mao-Lin hierarchy in Peking is striving to encourage cautious (or pragmatic) economic production rather than return to such wild Maoist schemes as the Great Leap Forward of 1958.

But it seems almost certain that some drastic political, social, economic, and cultural changes made during the Cultural Revolution will continue to be implemented. This will mean, for example, completing the take-over by the military, workers, and peasants of the management of schools; reshaping theatrical works to suit Maoist ideological requirements; and continuing the process of "re-educating" intellectuals, especially young Red Guard students, and subordinating them to workers and peasants.

In the sphere of foreign affairs, the post-Congress prospect appears to be a partial return to flexibility and pragmatism after the isolationist days of the Cultural Revolution. Nothing in the twenty-two years since the founding of the Chinese People's Republic has damaged the reputation of the Chinese Communists so severely as Mao's Cultural Revolution. During its height, in 1967 and even in 1968, Peking viewed the world only in simple ideological terms. Throughout the world, Communist China's supporters and sympathizers were utterly demoralized and even disgusted by Maoist revolutionary excesses. Between June 1966 and September 1967, Peking had been involved in quarrels of varying magnitude with thirty two countries. Only five foreign governments sent their customary delegations to the 1967 National Day (October 1) of Communist China: Albania, the Brazzaville Congo, Pakistan, Tanzania, and North Vietnam. Of the forty one nations around the world with which Peking maintained diplomatic relations headed by ambassadors, only one—the United Arab Republic —was graced by the presence of a Chinese Communist ambassador (Huang Hua) at his post. (Huang Hua was recalled in July 1968. In 1971 he was sent to Canada as Peking's ambassador.) The other forty ambassadors had been recalled at the start of the Cultural Revolution to undergo intensive reindoctrination in Mao's Thoughts, and repeated sessions of self-criticism. (When one ambassador to a non-Communist Asian country returned to Peking Airport, for example, he was compelled to kneel at the airport, bow to the Red Guards and other Maoist groups and confess that he had picked up bourgeois habits.) No Chinese Communist leader of stature had journeyed abroad since the spring of 1966. Recognition of Yemen and Mauritius and a sprinkling of economic aid projects— notably the Chinese Communist decision to build the Tanzania-Zambia and Mali-Guinea railroads—had been the most Peking could muster in the twelve months since the start of the Cultural Revolution.

Since April 1969, Communist China has been manifestly anxious to end the frightening diplomatic isolation imposed by the Cultural Revolution. The redeployment of Peking's ambassadors and senior diplomats began on May 16, 1969, when Keng Piao was dispatched to Albania as Communist China's new ambassador. Between then and the spring of 1971, the Mao-Lin regime had assigned twenty-nine ambassadors abroad to mend its diplomatic relations and to reassert its influence in world affairs. In addition, Peking has invited a strikingly varied group of foreign officials and delegates from abroad to discuss trade, aid, and improvement of relations, and most of them were treated to private audiences with the usually inaccessible Chairman Mao and his designated successor, Defense Minister Lin Piao. Audiences with Mao and Lin are supposed to represent the highest expression of Chinese support for foreign visitors to Peking. Premier Chou En-lai is expected to make an extensive goodwill tour abroad this year that will take him to the Middle East, Africa, and Europe. Chou's travels will climax a new departure in Chinese Communist diplomacy since the Cultural Revolution.

In recent months, Communist China has achieved diplomatic victories by establishing new diplomatic relations with Canada, Chile, Equatorial Guinea, Ethiopia, and Italy. In early 1971 Peking was considering diplomatic ties with Austria, Belgium, Bolivia, Ecuador, Iran, Lebanon, Libya, and Peru. As of March 1971, the Peking regime maintained formal diplomatic ties with fifty nation-states.[23] (It also had relations with the Cambodian exile regime of Prince Norodom Sihanouk and the provisional government set up by the Vietcong in South Vietnam.)

During 1969 the Sino-Soviet territorial dispute hovered on the brink of a major war between the two Communist giants, but the Mao-Lin regime resumed the boundary negotiations with the Soviet Union in October of the same year. In the fall of 1969 the two powers also agreed to exchange ambassadors, after having lacked them for nearly five years. When it came time to select its new ambassador to Moscow, Peking tapped Liu Hsin-chuan, a Deputy Foreign Minister, who was vilified by the Red Guards as a "bourgeois revisionist" during the height of the Cultural Revolution. (Vasily S. Tolstikov, the Communist Party leader for the Leningrad area, was named as Soviet ambassador to Peking.) After a period of treating their Russian adversaries with relative moderation, the Chinese Communists have recently emphasized their lack of interest in a Sino-Soviet rapprochement by resuming their propaganda denunciations of the Soviet Union.[24]

In late 1969, Peking resumed exploratory ambassadorial talks with the United States in Warsaw. (The American-Chinese ambassadorial talks in Warsaw were resumed in early 1970, but interrupted again in May 1970 when the Chinese canceled what would have been the 137th session, apparently because of President Nixon's dispatch of American troops to Cambodia.) Worried that the Soviet Union might launch a preemptive nuclear strike against the Chinese mainland, especially its nuclear establishment in Sinkiang, the Chinese Communists apparently embarked on a policy of countering Soviet threat wherever possible. It was also fearful of Washington-Moscow collusion, and even a possible joint attack by the two superpowers. For these reasons, Communist China hoped to play off Moscow against Washington within the newly emerging international political framework of the Moscow-Washington-Peking triangle. But hostilities with the United States remained unchanged in 1970. Condemning the recent American-South Vietnamese incursion into Laos, the Mao-Lin regime served a stern warning that it considered the incursion of Laos a "genuine menace to China," and said at the same time that Communist China could not remain indifferent to "such rabid acts of aggressions."[25] On April 8, 1971, however, Communist China suddenly responded to the Nixon Administration's amicable gestures toward normalizing diplomatic relations with Peking by inviting not only the American table tennis team participating in the Thirty-first World Table Tennis Tournament in Nagoya, Japan to play in Peking but also a number of American journalists. (It is significant to note that this invitation came in the middle of the Twenty-fourth Soviet Communist Party Congress, a meeting

Peking pointedly boycotted.) On April 14, 1971, Chinese Premier Chou En-lai received the American team, announcing that "a new page" was beginning in relations between the "Chinese and American people." In July, 1971, President Nixon was invited to visit Communist China before May 1972.

Since the Ninth Party Congress, the Peking regime has been attempting to improve its relations with the Communist countries of Eastern Europe and Asia in order to win a following in the Communist camp at the expense of the Soviet Union. Friendship with Communist China is an effective way for East European countries to demonstrate their independence from Moscow. Apart from the longtime Chinese ally of Albania, Peking's new diplomatic offensive has paid off most spectacularly in the two mavericks of Eastern Europe, Rumania and Yugoslavia. In April 1970, Premier Chou En-lai visited North Korea and rekindled a friendship with that Communist neighbor which had been almost snuffed out by Peking's anti Korean diatribes during the Cultural Revolution.[26] The invasion of Laos by South Vietnamese troops in early 1971 presented Communist China with another opportunity to boost its influence in North Vietnam. Again, Chou En-lai was the principal Chinese figure as he spent four days in Hanoi reassuring the North Vietnamese and receiving their thanks. On February 15, 1971, Peking signed an agreement with North Vietnam extending additional economic and military assistance in 1971.[27]

During the past few years, the Chinese Communists have sought to reassert their country's role as the leader of a third force and a champion of the lesser powers.[28] On July 12, 1970, for example, Communist China, Tanzania, and Zambia signed in Peking the loan agreement for building the Chinese-financed 1,100-mile Tanzania-Zambia railroad.[29] China's biggest single foreign aid project in Africa, this railroad stretches from Dar Es Salaam, the Tanzanian capital on the Indian Ocean, through the highlands and escarpment of southern Tanzania to Kapiri Mposhi on the rich copper belt of landlocked Zambia. The Chinese Communists are financing the project with a $400-million, interest-free loan that Tanzania and Zambia will pay back over thirty years, beginning in 1983.[30] (Already 4,700 Chinese are at work on the railroad alongside 7,000 Africans. The number of Chinese should reach 6,000 by the end of 1971). The construction of this railroad is scheduled to start in the fall of 1971 and expected to be completed in the mid-1970s.[31] The railroad project has political significance, for it is aimed partly at freeing black Zambia from its economic dependence on its white-ruled neighbors, Rhodesia and Portuguese Angola and Mozambique. At present, Zambia is forced to export most of its profitable copper through railroads in Rhodesia and Portuguese Angola. Tanzania will benefit from the trans-shipment of Zambian copper and it will be able to exploit the known coal and iron ore deposits in the south through which the projected railroad will run. Accordingly, the project, when completed, will give the Chinese Communists enormous presence and potential influence in an area that could become vital if there ever is a race war between white and black Africa.

In the sphere of foreign trade, the Chinese Communists in 1970 appeared to be moving to improve existing trade relations and seeking new trading partners. For all its bitter propaganda denunciations of the "imperialist" and capitalist West, Peking continues a flourishing and increasing trade with such countries as Great Britain and France. It trades heavily with some like Australia and West Germany without official diplomatic relations. Only in the case of Japan, collaborating with the Soviet Union in the development of Siberia, maintaining military alliance with the United States, and trading heavily with Nationalist China through official diplomatic relations, does Peking try to extract a pound of political flesh in its commercial dealings.[32]

In response to the Nixon Doctrine of gradual American troop withdrawals not only from Vietnam but from other Asian nations as well, Communist China has recently shifted some of its rhetorical abuse from the United States to Japan. Peking constantly sounds alarms that Japan is reviving its pre-World

War II militarism—with the support and encouragement of the United States.[33] The shift in Peking's rhetoric reflects Communist China's awareness that its future major rival in Asia will not be the United States, but Japan.

Despite all these efforts at returning to more pragmatic, more moderate forms of conducting foreign relations, the Chinese Communists have not shaken off all their Maoist militancy. That is to say, there still remain impressive remnants of the Cultural Revolution in Peking's post-Ninth Party Congress foreign policy. Peking's harsh verbal or propaganda abuse against the Soviet Union and the United States seems to have increased in 1970.[34] Communist China has recently overshadowed Soviet influence among the Asian Communists by vigorously supporting Prince Sihanouk's Cambodian government in exile. Just after the Vietnam war had spread to Cambodia in May 1970, it played host to a unity conference of all Indochinese Communists, and pledged strong Chinese Communist support until the war is won. The Mao-Lin regime continues to lend its support to Communist revolts against the governments of Thailand, Malaysia, Burma, Indonesia, and India. Peking has also championed "national liberation" movements in Africa by providing the black guerrillas in southern Tanzania with thousands of tons of arms and ammunition to be used in their forays into white-controlled Rhodesia, South Africa, and Portuguese Angola and Mozambique.[35] Denouncing the recent United States-sponsored Middle East peace proposal as a "political fraud" or "Munich scheme," Communist China has backed the Palestinian guerrillas, who are opposed to a truce with Israel, with arms and words.[36] The Chinese, apparently, are courting the Arab Palestinian guerrillas in an attempt to counteract Soviet influence with Arab governments. (Since the advent of the full-scale warfare between Jordanian troops and the Palestinian guerrillas in the fall of 1970 and the death of President Nasser in October 1970, Communist China has muted its public support for the Palestinian Liberation Organization and has taken steps to establish better state relations with many of the Arab governments, especially Egypt.)[37] The Chinese Communists support ongoing protracted conflict in the Middle East partly because they see the turmoil there as a chance to frustrate their main enemies, the United States and the Soviet Union, and partly because they desire to appear as the champion of world revolutionary forces.

In celebration of the twentieth anniversary of the founding of the Chinese People's Republic on October 1, 1969, meanwhile, the heavy emphasis was placed by the Mao-Lin regime not on further revolutionary upheaval or innovations, but on the need for greater unity, tighter Communist discipline (i. e., to combat anarchism and eliminate factionalism), increased production, and the consolidation of the ruling Maoist power structure.[38]

Judging from Peking's 1970 New Year statements and editorials, the prospect for Communist China in the foreseeable future seemed to be a continuation of vivid verbal pleas for "permanent revolution" combined with a sober effort to return to normalcy and stability.[39]

In the summer of 1970 when a series of steps were taken to rebuild the government apparatus following the disruptive effects of the Cultural Revolution, there were indications that the Peking leadership would try to convene a National People's Congress in the near future. On September 9, 1970, Peking announced that the Fourth National People's Congress would be held "at an appropriate time."[40] (The Third National People's Congress was elected in 1964 and met its first and only session from December 21, 1964, to January 4, 1965.) The decision to convene the new Congress was made at a plenary session of the Central Committee of the Chinese Communist Party, held from August 23 to September 6, 1970.

The National People's Congress, theoretically the highest organ of state authority, is, in practice, not a decision-making body but an instrument to put the rubber-stamp approval on whatever is submitted for its consideration by the Communist Party leadership. But its forthcoming meeting—at a date still undisclosed—will mark one more stage in the return to more orderly government since the Cultural Revolution. When it meets, the Congress is expected to adopt without dissent a new state constitution, and thereby bestow approval on the major changes in state structure implemented during the Cultural Revolution.

Reports have long been current that a draft state constitution has been circulating in Communist China for study by key officials. A copy of it was obtained by Chinese Nationalist authorities in Taiwan presumably through intelligence channels. The draft was released in Taipei on November 4, 1970 by the official Central News Agency of Nationalist China.[41] The Second Plenum of the Central Committee of the Chinese Communist Party in September 1970 reportedly approved a draft version of the new state constitution, and circulated it to lower levels for study and comment. The document is widely believed to be genuine, and this is reinforced by the fact that a draft of the new Chinese Communist Party Constitution, which surfaced outside Communist China under similar circumstances in early 1969, subsequently proved to be authentic.

Much shorter than the present constitution promulgated in 1954, the draft is also much less specific. While the present one contains 106 articles and 14,000 words, the new one has four chapters and 30 articles in a little more than 3,400 words, carrying the dominant mark of being uniquely for Mao Tse-tung and Maoism. The main characteristics of the new draft constitution are as follows:

1) The designation of Mao Tse-tung as "Great Leader of the People of All Nationalities, Head of State under the Dictatorship of the Proletariat and Supreme Commander of the Whole Nation and the Whole Army." His appointed successor, Lin Piao, is described as the "Close Comrade-in-Arms of and Successor to Chairman Mao and Deputy Supreme Commander of the Whole Nation and the Whole Army."[42]

2) The pre-eminent role of the Chinese Communist Party in Communist China: The dictatorship of the proletariat is to be exercised through the Party, of which Mr. Mao is the leader. (Mao thus combines state, Party and military dominance.) The National People's Congress can "revise the State Constitution, draw up the Constitution, or appoint or remove the Premier of the State Council" only "upon recommendation of the Central Committee of the Chinese Communist Party." (The 1954 State Constitution gave the Congress the independent power to amend the Constitution as well as officially to approve the appointment of the Premier upon the recommendation of the Chairman of the Chinese People's Republic.)

3) The National People's Congress is given a term of five instead of four years, as the case in the 1954 State Constitution.

4) The proclamation of Communist China as a "socialist state of proletarian dictatorship" (no longer a "people's democratic state," as described in the old Constitution), in which, however, the principle "to each according to his work" is to be enforced.

5) The description of Mao Tse-tung's Thought as "the guiding principle of all work carried out by the people of the whole country." "The most fundamental right and duty" of the Chinese people is to support Chairman Mao and his designated successor, Lin Piao.

6) The posts of chief of state (officially known as "President of the People's Republic of China" in the 1954 Constitution) and deputy chief of state will be abolished and the government's highest official will be the Premier, who heads the State Council. (Liu Shao-ch'i held the post of chief of state before he was purged during the Cultural Revolution.)

7) The Revolutionary Committees, which were established in Communist China's twenty-nine provinces as temporary agencies to replace government organs shattered during the Cultural Revolution, will be made a permanent part of the provincial government structure. And all governmental agencies must enforce the "three-way-alliance" (or "the revolutionary three-in-one com-

bination"). (The effect of this provision will be to certify the predominance of the Chinese People's Liberation Army in the provincial government bureaucracy of Communist China.)

It would seem likely that the Fourth National People's Congress will be convened after the rebuilding of the demolished Party organization throughout the country is completed.

NOTES TO CHAPTER 4

1. Press communiqué of the Secretariat of the Presidium of the Ninth Party Congress, April 1, 1969, in *Peking Review,* April 4, 1969, pp. 7–9.

2. *Ibid.*

3. For the full list of the 176 members of the Presidium of the Ninth Party Congress see *Peking Review,* April 30, 1969, p. 41.

4. For the full text of Lin Piao's report see *Peking Review,* April 30, 1969, pp. 16–35.

5. In early 1969, several calls were made again by some radical Maoists to begin another "Great Leap Forward" in 1969. See, for example, *Jenmin Jih-pao,* February 21, 1969.

6. This point indirectly reaffirmed Communist China's opposition to the peace talks in Paris. This tended to reinforce the impression that Peking's displeasure with North Vietnam had been growing in recent months over Hanoi's participation in peace talks with the United States. Although North Vietnam was one of the few nations to send a message of greeting to the Ninth Party Congress, neither Peking nor Lin's speech publicly thanked Hanoi by name or acknowledged the gesture.

7. Press communiqué of the Secretariat of the Presidium of the Ninth Party Congress, April 14, 1969, in *Peking Review,* April 30, 1969, pp. 42–43.

8. For the full text of the 1969 new Party Constitution see *Peking Review,* April 30, 1969, pp. 36–39.

9. Press communiqué of the Secretariat of the Presidium of the Ninth Party Congress, April 24, 1969, in *Peking Review,* April 30, 1969, pp. 44–47. For the list of the 279 regular and alternate members of the Ninth Central Committee see *ibid.,* pp. 47–48.

10. This announcement was included in Peking's report on a reception given by Chairman Mao and Vice-Chairman Lin for 10,000 military representatives in Peking. *New China News Agency,* May 20, 1969.

11. The Eighth Central Committee of the Chinese Communist Party had roughly twenty-five per cent military men among both the regulars and alternates.

12. See *Peking Review,* April 30, 1969, pp. 48–49.

13. The old Eighth Politburo originally had twenty regular members and six alternates. During the Cultural Revolution, however, it was enlarged through the addition of Nieh Jung-chen, Hsu Hsiang-chien, Yeh Chien-ying, Hsieh Fu-chih, and Li Hsueh-feng.

14. The highest-ranking woman in Communist China before the Cultural Revolution was Soong Ching-ling, widow of Dr. Sun Yat-sen, the father of the Chinese Republic. Although she was one of the two deputy heads of state, her political influence was never significant. In 1968, she was harassed and denounced by the Red Guards. She has not made any public appearance in recent months.

15. See *Who's Who in Communist China* (Hong Kong: Union Research Institute, 1966), pp. 553–554, 563–565.

16. *Peking Review,* April 30, 1969, p. 43. There were no differences in substance between the final text and the draft, although the Constitution adopted by the Ninth Congress contained changes in phraseology and some additions of paragraphs and sentences as compared with the draft Party charter.

17. Peter J. Kumpa's dispatch from Hong Kong, in *The* (Baltimore) *Sun,* April 27, 1969, p. 1.

18. *Peking Review,* April 30, 1969, p. 42.

19. *Ibid.*

20. Press communiqué of the Secretariat of the Presidium of the Ninth Party Congress, April 24, 1969, in *Peking Review,* April 30, 1969, p. 45.

21. *New China News Agency,* May 20, 1969.

22. See footnote 10 of this chapter.

23. They were: Afghanistan, Burma, Ceylon, India, Iraq, Laos, Nepal, North Korea, North Vietnam, Outer Mongolia, Pakistan, Syria, Yemen, South Yemen, Albania, Great Britain, Czechoslovakia, Denmark, East Germany, Finland, France, Hungary, Italy, the Netherlands, Norway, Poland, Rumania, the Soviet Union, Sweden, Switzerland, Yugoslavia, Algeria, the Brazzaville Congo, Guinea, Equatorial Guinea, Ethiopia, Kenya, Mali, Mauritania, Morocco, Nigeria, Somalia, the Sudan, Tanzania, Uganda, the United Arab Republic, Zambia, Cuba, Chile, and Canada. Seven countries recognized but did not have diplomatic relations with Communist China—Tunisia, Ghana, Burundi, Senegal, Indonesia, Israel and Mauritius.

24. See *Peking Review,* March 19, 1971, pp. 3–13.

25. See *Peking Review,* January 29, 1971, pp. 5–9; February 12, 1971, pp. 5–7; February 26, 1971, p. 6; March 5, 1971, p. 17; and March 12, 1971, pp. 15–21.

26. See Robert R. Simmons, "The Peking-Pyongyang-Moscow Triangle," *Current Scene,* November 1970, pp. 8–18; and *Peking Review,* April 10, 1970, pp. 3–14; May 8, 1970, pp. 3–4; May 15, 1970, pp. 3–4; and May 22, 1970, p. 3.

27. *Peking Review,* March 12, 1971, pp. 4–21.

28. See Joseph D. Ben-Dak, "China in the Arab World," *Current History*, September 1970, pp. 147–152; *Free China Weekly*, Taipei, Formosa, February 21, 1971, p. 2; *The New York Times*, January 10, 1971, p. 7; February 10, 1971, p. 9; February 26, 1971, p. 23; *The Los Angeles Times*, November 6, 1970, p. 5; and *The Washington Post*, February 26, 1971, p. 23.

29. *Peking Review*, July 17, 1970, pp. 16–17.

30. *The* (Baltimore) *Sun*, July 13, 1970, p. 1; *The Los Angeles Times*, November 1, 1970, p. 2 (Section G); *The New York Times*, November 8, 1970, p. 6 (E); and *The Washington Post*, November 10, 1970, p. 33. Aside from this railroad loan, Tanzania was also given $60 million of economic assistance in the past. *The Los Angeles Times*, June 16, 1970, p. 2.

31. Since the original railroad agreement was signed in Peking in 1967, Chinese Communist engineers, technicians and workers had been surveying and designing the railroad. This work was completed in April 1970.

32. See *Peking Review*, March 12, 1971, pp. 24–25; and Walter LaFeber, "China and Japan: Different Beds, Different Dreams," *Current History*, September 1970, pp. 142–146. Japan's trade with Taiwan is larger than its trade with mainland China. Total turnover in 1970 reached $900 million with Taiwan and $825 million with Communist China. See *The New York Times*, March 31, 1971, p. 14.

33. See *Jen-min Jih-pao*, October 24, 1970; November 1, 1970; December 4, 1970; and *Peking Review*, January 22, 1971, pp. 11–13; and January 29, 1971, pp. 20–21.

34. See, for example, "Leninism or Social-Imperialism?" the joint editorial of *Jen-min Jih-pao*, *Hung Ch'i*, and *Chieh-fang-chün Pao*, April 22, 1970, in *Peking Review*, April 24, 1970, pp. 5–14; and Mao Tse-tung, "People of the World, Unite and Defeat the U.S. Aggressors and All Their Running Dogs!" May 20, 1970, in *Peking Review*, May 23, 1970, pp. 8–9.

35. *The New York Times*, November 8, 1970, p. 6 (E); and *The Washington Post*, February 26, 1971, p. 23.

36. *The Washington Post*, September 16, 1970, p. 27.

37. *Ibid.*, February 6, 1971, p. 16.

38. See the full text of Lin Piao's speech at the rally celebrating the twentieth anniversary of the birth of the Chinese People's Republic, in *Peking Review*, October 3, 1969, pp. 15–16; *Hung Ch'i*, October 1, 1969; and *Jen-min Jih-pao*, October 1, 1969.

39. *Jen-min Jih-pao*, January 1, 1970; and *Chieh-fang-chün Pao*, January 1, 1970.

40. *New China News Agency*, September 9, 1970.

41. See *Background on China*, B. 70–81, November 4, 1970; *Current Scene*, December 7, 1970, pp. 18–19; *The New York Times*, November 6, 1970, p. 3; and *The Washington Post*, November 6, 1970, p. 16. The following discussion of the new draft constitution of Communist China is based on these sources.

42. On October 1, 1970, the twenty-first anniversary of the Communist rule in mainland China, Chairman Mao received the new title "Supreme Commander of the Whole Nation and the Whole Army." His deputy, Lin Piao, was designated as "Deputy Supreme Commander of the Whole Nation and the Whole Army." *New China News Agency,* October 1, 1970.

CHAPTER 5

Evaluation

FIVE YEARS after Chairman Mao launched his last and desperate campaign to carry out the militant rectification of the sagging Communist revolution in China, it is apparent that h'' Cultural Revolution is a failure. Despite all the extra propaganda extolling his "great victory," Mao h attain the three important objectives of the Cultural Revolution. The Cultural Revolution still continues in a more orderly fashion, but it is only a verbally radical propaganda campaign, its original goals unreached and set aside. "The Chinese are," as Robert S. Elegant says, "no less adept than other peoples [of the world] at saying one thing while actually doing not quite the opposite—perhaps more adept."[1]

As stated previously, the first goal of the Cultural Revolution had the twin objectives of (a) smashing the entire Communist Party dominated by "revisionist" leaders and (b) of reforming and revitalizing it entirely with loyal Maoist "revolutionary rebels." Chairman Mao succeeded over the past five years in discrediting and purging his so-called "revisionist" opponents within the entire Communist Party apparatus; to this extent, he is surely the winner. (Purged former top Communists were not executed, imprisoned or sent to labor camps but were placed under house arrest in different villas in the

suburbs of Peking.)[2] But the power seized from these opponents, instead of passing to his Proletarian Headquarters in
Peking and to the radical "rebel" partisans in the provinces,
was taken over for the most part by the army (especially local
military officers), intent on restoring law and order by curbing
the excesses that threatened to fragment the country; in this
sense, Mao can be called the loser. In short, Mao's success in
achieving the first goal of the Cultural Revolution is largely
superficial, and a partial or Pyrrhic victory at best.

Mao's Cultural Revolution has given the Chinese People's
Liberation Army the most extensive control over the Chinese
mainland since the Communists seized power twenty-two years
ago. The military did not grab power in a swift coup, but
rather was brought into the center of the political stage by
Chairman Mao to bring law and order out of the chaos of his
wild Cultural Revolution, and power gradually gravitated to
it. The major legacy of the Cultural Revolution is military
dominance of government and Communist Party affairs.

The army is today the only nationwide organization still
functioning with enough organizational integrity and discipline
to preserve the stability, unity and integrity of the nation, although it too shows signs of internal disagreements or divisions
along regional, generational, doctrinal, and service lines. The
military has assumed a significant political role in Communist
China, with its high-ranking officers holding key positions in
the central and provisional organs of power. In addition, lesser
army officers and troops supervise industry, agriculture, railways, education, and nearly every other sector of the country.
Soldiers are even the authors or heroes of numerous press
articles. Peking today remains the symbolic capital, or a pa-
per tiger, and military men who now wield real authority
primarily as chairmen or vice-chairmen of most of the provincial-level Revolutionary Committees are adopting pragmatic
policies while pretending total obedience to Mao's revolutionary
ideology.

The fastest rising man in the national leadership in the past several years is Army Chief of Staff Huang Yung-sheng, who now ranks fifth on official lists and is believed to be the second most powerful military man in China after Defense Minister Lin Piao. (As Commander of the Canton Military Region in the turbulent summer of 1967, "General" Huang was one of the first army officers to speak out against the excesses of the Cultural Revolution and to order his troops to open fire on the young Maoist fanatics, according to a Chinese language newspaper in Hong Kong reported February 23, 1971. Meanwhile, Huang was injured in an assassination attempt on February 10, 1971 in Kwangtung Province.[3])

Indications are that the army is intent upon consolidating and extending its political power through the Revolutionary Committees and the new Party organizations in Communist China's twenty-nine provinces, and shows no great hurry to relinquish its dominant political role, despite the heavier burden of defense preparedness it is now carrying as a result of the danger of major war with the Soviet Union along the 4,150-mile Sino-Soviet boundary. For example, on August 1, 1969, "General" and Army chief of Staff Huang Yung-sheng said publicly that the army's supervision of the nation's daily life would continue.[4] This speech was made in the presence of an array of Peking's top Party leaders and military officers at a reception held to celebrate the forty-second anniversary of the founding of the Chinese Communist armed forces.

Thus after two decades, Communist China finds itself in a position where Chairman Mao's most venerated principle has been spectacularly overturned. Mao's dictum was that "power grows out of the barrel of a gun,"[5] and, viewed in perspective, this maxim has still proved correct. But his injunction that "the Party commands the gun, and the gun will never be allowed to command the Party"[6] is now operating in reverse. This is admitted openly. For example, Lin Piao said in his opening speech to the Ninth Party Congress that the army was "the mighty pillar of the dictatorship of the proletariat" and the "main component of the state."[7]

Today the military dominates the political scene in most of Communist China's twenty-nine provinces. But the great majority of the twenty-nine provincial-level Revolutionary Committees that have replaced the demolished Party and government bodies throughout the country are having much difficulty in achieving a balance of unity and managerial efficiency,[8] for they are based on unstable or hostile coalitions of representatives of the rival Maoist "rebel" organizations, including radical leftists and rightists, old Party officials who have survived the Cultural Revolution, and a strong element of the army men. The rival Maoist "rebel" elements continue to bicker and feud over vendettas, seeking a settling of "old accounts";[9] former civilian Party officials are still unwilling to reassert their power for fear of being assaulted again by the Maoist revolutionary left, which continues to challenge the "rehabilitation" of these formerly disgraced veteran apparatchiks; and radical-minded Maoist "rebels" and the seasoned Party officials are unable to co-exist peacefully, far less work together effectively, thus leaving the army as the only functioning provincial leadership. But the military lacks governmental experience and expertise.

In many provinces the army has forged a "conservative" two-way alliance with old Party officials against the Maoist leftists, although they pay lip service to the "three-way revolutionary alliance" on which the present power structure of the Revolutionary Committee is ostensibly based. This has led the Maoist radical elements, who were given a token share of power in the new Revolutionary Committees, to become the chief opponents of the new "conservative" power structure. They have been agitating for a greater share of power, even in defiance of Peking's pleas for unity.[10]

On the eve of Communist China's 1970 Army Day (August 1), a Maoist-controlled Shanghai broadcast challenged the dominant role of the army in the political and administrative life of the country.[11] Shanghai is one area in which the power base of Maoist radicals remains strong and is the outstanding exception to military dominance. It is the headquarters of Chang Chun-chiao and Yao Wen-yuan, who came to political prominence during the Cultural Revolution, in close association with Chiang Ching. Three personalities, all members of the new ruling Party Politburo, constitute the central core of Maoist radical thinking. The Shanghai broadcast carried a series of quotations on the proper role of the army taken from the works of Mao Tse-tung, and said: "The people's armed forces of a Socialist country must always be placed under the leadership of the political party of the proletariat and the supervision of the masses of the people."[12] This statement obliquely called into question the present situation in which the army exerted dominant political influence beyond its former jurisdiction and blocked the Maoist radical groups from gaining power.

Vigorous defense of the army role came immediately from the provinces of Hupeh and Honan. A broadcast from Hupeh praised the efforts of the army in having "protected the Revolutionary Committees at all levels and helped them with their ideological revolution."[13] The army-dominated Revolutionary Committees were, it said, the new provincial administrative bodies based on the "three-way revolutionary alliance."[14]

Discussing the army's role, a Honan broadcast asserted that it was important that the army made sure that its guns would be forever "in the hands of people profoundly loyal to Chairman Mao."[15]

Persistent agitation by radical Maoist "rebel" organizations is hobbling the efforts of Communist China's provincial authorities to create a stable political situation. The agitation has recently led to serious new clashes in some provinces between various rival Maoist "rebel" factions, and between the radical-minded Maoists on the one hand and the army or civilian supporters of Party officials in power on the other.[16]

The combined moderate or conservative forces of military leaders and old Party officials have strengthened their positions in the provinces by ruthlessly purging Maoist leftists from posts in the Revolutionary Committees and even from the mass organizations. What was worse, some confirmed Maoist radicals in provincial power, who had enjoyed the patronage of Mao Tse-tung and his wife, Chiang Ching, were losing their power to moderate-minded military officers in recent months.

The current trend toward institutionalization and stability has worked inexorably against the radical Maoist left. In the spring of 1970, there were changes in the top leadership of Shantung, Shansi, and Kweichow, with a loss of position for Maoist radicals.[17] (Before this, the originally Maoist-oriented Heilungkiang Provincial Revolutionary Committee was already shaking off its previous radicalism.)[18] In these cases, law-and-order-minded military officers gained decisive power at the expense of the earliest and most ardent supporters of the Cultural Revolution. In the case of Shantung Province, Wang Hsiao-yu, the leader of the Maoist "revolutionary rebels" in the province, who became Chairman of the Shantung Provincial Revolutionary Committee when it was set up on February 3, 1967, was purged, and Yang Teh-chih, commander of the Tsinan Military Region, and Yuan Sheng-ping, deputy political commissar of the same region, took over leadership of the Committee.[19] Wang's downfall was followed by a thorough reorganization in the province from top to bottom to root out the leftist "rebels" and all those who gained office on the Maoist "rebel" seizure of power in February 1967 totally disappeared from recent provincial gatherings.[20] In the case of the Shansi Provincial Revolutionary Committee, Liu Ke-ping was removed as Chairman, and Chang Jih-ching Vice-Chairman.[21] The Kweichow Provincial Revolutionary Committee came under moderate army control after its former Maoist chairman, Li Tsai-han, was purged in early 1970.[22]

Some top-ranking Maoist extremists, who gathered around Mme. Mao and thus held sway during the height of the Cultural Revolution, have not been seen in public for months. One of them is Chen Po-ta, the fourth-ranking member of the Chinese hierarchy and an ideological architect of the Cultural Revolution. (Mr. Chen has not appeared at public occasions since August 1970.) Reasons behind his political disappearance are not yet clear. Some speculate that he is now in disgrace. According to the January 9, 1971 issue of the Hong Kong *Star*, however, Chen was not purged but is receiving medical care for angina pectoris and an ear complaint.

Despite the above events, the radical Maoist elements, of whom Chiang Ching is an acknowledged leader, do not yet appear to be a clear and final loser in the factional power struggle. They are still a factional force very much to be reckoned with by the moderates. The stress, recently revived in the Maoist press and radio, on contributions made by Mme. Mao in the cultural field indicates that her influence—and the support she receives from her husband—are formidable.

The present pressure for a bigger share of power by the Maoist "rebel" leftists has grown and intensified in conjunction with the current nationwide movement to rebuild the demolished Communist Party apparatus, which started right after the Ninth Party Congress. The revolutionary leftists feel that they have earned a strong claim to a significant political role in the new Party structure by destroying the old Party establishment dominated by the "bourgeois enemies of the people," in enthusiastic compliance with Chairman Mao's aim of bringing vigorous new "revolutionary successors" into leadership roles. They have had violent disagreements with the provincial powerholders (the army) over the question of what sort of persons should be entitled to join and lead the renovated Party. In their opinion, they deserve the majority representation in the new Party machine in order to prevent it from slipping back onto Liu Shao-ch'i's "reactionary" road again.

Mao and his radical wing of the Peking Proletarian Headquarters have recently made a new move to help the Maoist revolutionary leftists gain control in the emerging new Party organs in the provinces.[23] They apparently hope to strengthen their hands and thus reassert their influence in the new Party structure and national affairs by placing their loyal supporters in new key Party positions. Mao's instruction to "exhale the old and inhale the new" provided the Maoist radicals with good ammunition in their attempt to purge the old Party members once more and to hamper the provincial authorities' plan to rehabilitate and accept these previously purged or disgraced Party officials into the new Party power structure.

But the military leaders now controlling most of the country's twenty-nine provinces, who are determined to ensure their predominance in Party and administrative organs, seek to ignore Mao's instruction through a purge of leftists from the Party and rehabilitation of the old moderate Party members. They defend the rehabilitated Party members against leftist attempts to "drag them out" once again, contending that "the overwhelming majority of them are willing to follow Chairman Mao in continuing the revolution."[24]

This has triggered further tensions between the moderate-minded provincial powerholders and the Maoist fanatics and led to widespread unrest throughout the country. Unable to have their own way, the Maoist "rebels" have tried to sabotage "conservative" attempts to rebuild the Party, even by raising the fundamental question of whether the reconstruction of Party organizations is desirable. In some provinces where the Maoist ideologues have been heavily defeated, they contend that it is sufficient to have only the leadership of Mao's Thought, so no Party committees or Party branches are necessary.[25] They maintain that the new Party organizations which have been created by a "conservative" coalition of military officers and the old Party members do not represent the true Party, and have no paramount power over other organizations.[26] This view is in turn severely denounced by the military powerholders in the provinces, who claim that leadership by the Party is indispensable, that Party organizations at all levels represent the Party itself and are therefore entitled to exercise absolute authority.[27] The Maoist extremists are accused of "doubledealing," of paying lip service to Maoism but of not implementing it.[28]

By and large, the power struggle between the radical leftists and their moderate opponents has found a new battleground in the reconstruction of the Chinese Communist Party. The intensity of this struggle had caused the process of Party re-building in the provinces to proceed at a snail's pace in 1969 and 1970. Out of Communist China's 2,000 counties, less than one hundred were believed to have reconstructed their Party committees by the end of 1970, and no Party committees had yet been formed at the provincial level until mid-December 1970.[29]

The Mao-Lin regime in Peking has failed to provide any clearcut guidelines to settle the dissension, possibly because of policy conflicts within Mao's Proletarian Headquarters, or perhaps out of reluctance to clarify issues that divide the moderate and radical elements. For example, the guideline given by Peking on July 1, 1969, the forty-eighth anniversary of the founding of the Chinese Communist Party, was that the newly emerging Party organs in the provinces (and lower levels) must be formed "gradually" and according to the "concrete conditions" of each province.[30] Such a vague guideline has given the provincial authorities considerable room to maneuver, and thus encouraged them to ignore Peking's call for the active participation of the Maoist leftists in Party reconstruction and to act in an increasingly independent and arbitrary manner, with a consequent weakening of the Mao-Lin regime's effective political control outside Peking.

On the question of relationship between reconstructed Party organs and the present Revolutionary Committees at all levels of administration, Chairman Mao asserts that the latter are subordinate to the former.[31] In other words, power will eventually be transferred from the Revolutionary Committees to the new Party organs. His notion of forming a "strong core of Party leadership" in the Revolutionary Committees throughout the country indicates that he wants to reassert Party power all over Communist China by establishing a strong Party structure, which will give him and his Proletarian Headquarters more effective control than it now can exert through the present loosely knit arrangement of Revolutionary Committees.

But there have been indications that in many provinces the army-dominated Revolutionary Committees are not enthusiastic about seeing Party branches (or committees) develop that would encroach upon their newly gained authority. Accordingly, the military officers dominating most of the provinces are attempting to convert, or already are converting, the Revolutionary Committees into provincial Party branches through an overlapping of membership—which logically means the formalization of military predominance in the reconstructed Party.

In short, the prime mover in the Party-rebuilding process in most of the country's provinces is the army. (The Revolutionary Committees in the provinces are now fulfilling the function of electoral colleges for Party membership.) The military will be able to assert enough muscle to end infighting and impose order in recalcitrant areas. Such action would parallel the stepped-up military role in forming Revolutionary Committees in the later stages of the Cultural Revolution.

The reorganization of the Chinese Communist Party at the provincial level has picked up speed since late December 1970. It was generally believed in Hong Kong that the Mao-Lin regime wanted to complete party rebuilding in all twenty-nine administrative areas in time for the fiftieth anniversary celebration of the Party's founding on July 1, 1971.[32] Official Chinese Communist announcements had hinted at such a goal, but the Mao-Lin regime had stopped short of publicly setting itself a deadline.

By August 26, 1971, Communist China completed the process of rebuilding the demolished old Party apparatus at province level.[33] (A long-awaited meeting of the Fourth National People's Congress may follow soon, probably before the end of 1971.) The military retains its predominance in the majority of all the provincial-level Party committees. More specifically, of 158 leaders—first secretaries, second secretaries and deputy secretaries—59.5 per cent are military men, 34.8 per cent are veteran civilian Party cadres and 5.7 per cent are Maoist revolutionary radicals.[34] (All the Party committees are headed by chairmen of the provincial-level Revolutionary Committees as first secretaries, twenty of whom are the military officers. Some original chairmen of the Revolutionary Committees are now in disgrace, so they have also lost leadership of their provincial-level Party committees.)[35] This clearly represents a victory for the moderate-pragmatist leadership group over the radical "vanguards" of the Cultural Revolution. More important, the renovated Chinese Communist Party machine is, instead of "commanding the gun," controlled by the gun.

As for the second goal of the Cultural Revolution—that of training and developing new young Maoist "revolutionary heirs" through an ideological revolution and, subsequently, injecting them into the revamped organs of power at all levels— the evidence suggests that Chairman Mao has failed to achieve this goal.

Before the Cultural Revolution started, Mao deplored that Communist China's young generation, who "had not suffered in the old society and lacked experience in class struggle," had joined the Party for the sake of prestige and position only since the establishment of the Chinese People's Republic in 1949. One of Mao's reasons for launching the Cultural Revolution was to develop a generation that would be dedicated to his militant Communist goals and to insure that they would not turn into bureaucrats or "revisionists" mindful of the status quo and material comforts.

In the early stage of the Cultural Revolution, the young Red Guards and other Maoist "revolutionary rebels" appeared to be enthusiastic in support of Mao's siren call for "rebellion" against the old and mellowed Party establishment. But no sooner had Mao's "revolutionary successors" destroyed an aging Party bureaucracy dominated by anti-Mao "revisionist" opponents, than they began to fight each other for power and positions instead of remolding Chinese society in the image of

Mao's Utopian ideology, and the country was thrown into chaos and anarchy.

As the past course of the Cultural Revolution clearly indicates, much—perhaps most—of Communist China's young generation appears to be individualistic, selfish, and corruptible. "If this is indeed the case," as Stanley Karnow astutely observes, "then the Cultural Revolution was doomed to ultimate failure even before it started." For the very generation Mao counted on to carry his militant revolution through to the end after his death has turned out to be almost instinctively "bourgeois" and "revisionist." That is to say, Mao's Cultural Revolution has ironically fallen a victim to the very brand of base human behavior he sought to eradicate.

The Cultural Revolution consumed its own children or "vanguards" too soon. Beginning in the fall of 1968, most of Mao's young "revolutionary successors" have, with the Chairman's assent, been systematically crushed as "counter-revolutionaries" by a new Chinese bureaucracy composed of a "conservative" two-way alliance of military officers and old Party apparatchiks. In anniversary-conscious China, August 18, the date of the political debut of the Red Guards, is no longer a day of widespread celebration. As punishment for their rampant factional activities in the past, millions of young ex-Red Guard students have been forcibly shipped to remote rural and frontier regions on the pretext that they will become imbued with a true "proletarian spirit" by working as peasants or manual laborers. Many leaders of the Red Guards and other Maoist extremists have been arrested, brought before so-called "people's tribunals," and publicly executed.

Along with this, a vast campaign known as "hsia fang," or "down to the countryside," is being intensified. Since the Cultural Revolution began in 1966, about 40 million students, teachers, workers, doctors, and other urban residents have been sent down to rural areas. Mass shipment of students and urban residents to remote rural and frontier areas serves many useful purposes for the Mao-Lin regime: (a) to eradicate the traditional differences existing in China between the peasant masses and the intellectuals, between the cities and the countryside, and between mental and manual labor; (b) to relieve congestion in the overpopulated cities, where unemployment pressures and food distribution problems are extensive; and (c) to strengthen Communist China's defense along the border with the Soviet Union.

Young ex-Red Guard students who somehow managed to remain in urban areas have been compelled to submit to harsh discipline and controls by squads of soldiers and workers. Reports have appeared recently in the Maoist press of restlessness and discontent among young people in the countryside and of a reluctance among those still in the cities to accept rural assignments.[36] Many Chinese youths, dissatisfied with the hard life in the countryside and with their lack of opportunity, have illegally drifted back to the cities, where they reportedly live in an underworld, engaging in activities ranging from blackmarketeering to prostitution.[37] Many of the former Red Guards have recently risked death by drowning or from the guns of border guards to make the five-mile swim to the British Crown Colony of Hong Kong. By and large, millions of young Chinese, astray in the cities or shipped to remote rural and frontier areas, today constitute a lost generation, and are growing into one of Peking's prime headaches.

Undoubtedly, the great majority of millions of the young ex-Red Guard students are angry with the deceit and hypocrisy of the Mao-Lin leadership which cynically used their youthful idealism to overthrow its "revisionist" opponents—and which has now left them in the lurch. They blame Mao openly for having deceived and doublecrossed them, and react with resentment and occasional violence to their recent humiliation and present ordeal of repression and punishment. Many of them are also weary and cynical of the rhetoric and turbulence of the Cultural Revolution. Accordingly, the possibility cannot entirely be ruled out that, if pushed to the wall, they may provoke fresh violence throughout the country, even against Communist China's demi-God—Chairman Mao. After all, a spirit of rebellion against authority of any kind, including the authority of the Proletarian Headquarters in Peking, is one important legacy the Cultural Revolution has left to the young Chinese people. Young intellectuals and students have been the most volatile elements in modern Chinese history.

Meanwhile, the campaign to rebuild and revitalize the discredited Chinese Youth Communist League into a reservoir of loyal Maoist successors and aides to the existing hierarchy seems to be gaining momentum slowly in mainland China.[38] As of this writing, it is not clear what role, if any, the young ex-Red Guard militants will play in the revived Communist Youth League. But it seems likely that the newly formed Party committees in the provinces will guide and dominate the League as an effective instrument for controlling Communist China's young population.

As of now, Mao's failure to make progress toward the third goal of the Cultural Revolution—that of eliminating all "feudal" and "bourgeois" as well as "revisionist" influences among the Chinese people—is clear. Mao's Cultural Revolution has failed to destroy what Maoist dogma calls the "four olds"— old ideas, old culture, old customs, and old habits. Five years after the advent of the Cultural Revolution, he finds that the "old civilization" he swore to destroy remains unbroken. The Chinese people are traditionally conservative and pragmatic, and tend to resist with deep stubbornness or skillful resourcefulness any sudden radical changes in their proud 5,000-year-old civilization.

Maoist attempts to "revolutionize" the traditional family (or "put Mao Tse-tung Thought in command of the whole family") by replacing the old ties, loyalties and interests by desired Socialist attitudes have come to no avail. The Mao-Lin regime is opposed to the traditional Chinese family unit as a potential source of resistance, and as an obstacle to Communist objectives. However, family ties, superstitious beliefs, and traditions die hard, especially in the rural areas of the Chinese mainland. Despite numerous reports in the press and radio in recent months of "revolutionized" families that take Mao Tse-tung Thought as the supreme criterion for the conduct of whole family members,[39] it is probable that, if they really exist at all, they are "models" which are far from being representative of the average family of the mainland.

There are today both widespread civil disobedience and passive resistance to unpopular collectivist policies favored by Mao. The Chinese people are displaying the very opposite of revolutionary spirit in their passive opposition to the removal of existing material incentive systems such as piecework and private plots, which were introduced as a conciliatory gesture after the disastrous Great Leap Forward and the communes of 1958 had alienated the peasants and also adversely affected production.[40]

Even many provincial authorities ruled by the moderate-minded army officers have once again given their official blessing to the private plot and other material incentives, dismissing Mao's romantic and Utopian notion of spiritual incentives simply as impractical for inspiring the "enthusiasm of the masses" to win the "battle of raising agriculture and industrial production."[41]

The Mao-Lin regime in Peking continues to pay lip service to the Maoist economic dogma that denounces the heresy of material incentives, but recently there has been a marked shift to a more pragmatic way of thinking.[42] A series of articles in the Maoist publications in Peking have given formal approval to a broad range of incentives, which have proved not only popular with the peasants but also a stimulus to higher productivity. For example, a *Jen-min Jih-pao* editorial of March 22, 1969 warned against any change in the present ownership and other material incentive systems in the rural communes. The new draft state constitution, which is expected to be approved in the near future by the forthcoming Fourth National People's Congress, specifically protects a citizen's right to farm private plots of land. Even the use of material incentives to encourage hard work has appeared under the guise of "rational rewards."

Indeed, the irony of Mao's radical Cultural Revolution in its fifth year is that the entire country continues with an orgy of hate against Liu Shao-ch'i, denounced daily as a "renegade, scab, traitor, agent of the Kuomintang, and China's Khrushchev," but some of his favorite "revisionist" policies are being followed.

According to official reports from Peking and a dozen provinces, black market operations, corruption, theft, embezzlement, and other acts of opposition to the Maoist social order have become once more a major problem throughout the country. The military-led provincial authorities in southern China staged large numbers of mass trials and public executions in the spring and summer of 1970 in an apparent effort to curb an assortment of criminal and "counter-revolutionary" offenses and to restore social order.[43] A large proportion of the many hundreds recently tried and executed in Kwangtung Province for various alleged crimes were young people. Many of them were ex-Red Guard students who had rebelled against being sent to work in the countryside and had turned to crime to feed themselves.[44]

Apparently equally disturbing to the Mao-Lin regime is the continuing rise of "bourgeois" individualism, widespread public apathy, despair, and cynicism among workers, peasants, students, officials, and even soldiers, who are clearly tired of years of agonizing political pressure and rigorous ideological drives. All in all, the past five-year course of the Cultural Revolution dramatizes the failure of Mao's dream to create a perfect Socialist society of a new species of human beings who are selfless, disciplined, doggedly industrious, and willing to live and die for collectivist goals in the spirit of self-abnegation.

As of this writing, in short, the Cultural Revolution is finished as a forward movement. And the aftereffects of the near-anarchy it triggered in the past are still being felt in

Communist China's economic, educational, and social spheres.

The upheavals of the Cultural Revolution had adversely affected Communist China's economic performance.[45] There had been a definite stagnation in industrial and agricultural production, foreign trade, and other areas of the economy during the height of Mao's convulsive Cultural Revolution.

Since the convocation of the Ninth Party Congress in April 1969, Communist China has turned to the arduous task of economic reconstruction. Resisting the temptation to embark on another Great Leap Forward with its fatal emphasis on heavy industry, the country has continued patiently to build up agriculture as the foundation of the nation's economic development and the medium and small industries connected with it.[46] Although Peking's blackout on economic statistics makes outside evaluation difficult or impossible, it is apparent that mainland China made significant progress in 1970 toward restoring and revitalizing an economy shaken by the Cultural Revolution.[47] And the outlook for economic growth in 1971 is believed to be more promising than they had been for a decade.[48]

Peking's overall industrial production apparently recovered in 1969 possibly to the 1966 level of the pre-Cultural Revolution.[49] Industrial production in 1970 reportedly was not only higher than in 1966 but reached the record level attained in 1959.[50] New construction is seen in the cities, oil supplies seem adequate, manufactured goods and ordinary consumer commodities seem to be in better supply (although the society boasts little luxury), and railways and shipping are operating at capacity.[51]

Communist China's grain output for 1969 was believed to be around 190 million metric tons, as compared to 180 to 185 million calculated as the grain total for 1968 and 190 million for 1967.[52] The country continued to import 4.5 million metric tons of wheat from Canada, Australia, and other countries in 1969, and it cost Peking $305 million.[53] Peking's total grain output in 1970 reportedly was possibly 210 million metric tons or more.[54] The harvest in 1970 was the ninth consecutive good harvest, which was made possible in large measure by an unusual absence of major droughts or floods during that period.[55]

In 1969, Peking's two-way foreign trade volume reached about $3.9 billion, five per cent above 1968, but still some eight per cent below the 1966 level (see *Tables* 3 and 4). In the same year, Peking established the favorable trade balance with a comfortable $235 million surplus of exports over imports (see *Table* 4). It was predicted by foreign trade sources in Hong Kong that the 1970 trade level would be close to, and perhaps top, the 1966 level.[56]

Both on October 1, 1969, and January 1, 1971, the Mao-Lin regime had announced that the Third Five-Year Plan, begun in 1966, had been "successfully fulfilled," but no details were given of the goals achieved.[57] At the same time, it had disclosed that the Fourth Five-Year Plan, to begin in 1971, is being drawn up to be adopted at the forthcoming National People's Congress.[58] But again no details were given of any priorities or goals for the fourth plan.

Despite a general improvement in the domestic economy, the Chinese economy is not without some serious problems. Many enterprises suffer from labor laxity and poor management. Much capital equipment was damaged during the Cultural Revolution by strikes, strife, and sabotage. Even more damaging to Communist China's industry was the effect of the dispersion of skilled labor, managers, and technicians. In 1970, capital accumulation and investment appeared to be desperately slow. The gross national product probably has now reached the 1966 level, but an annual population growth of 15 to 20 million will certainly aggravate existing economic problems of the country.

Mao's dogmatic Cultural Revolution also had a damaging effect on the morale and efficiency of Communist China's scientific community, which holds the chief responsibility for Peking's technological development and modernization. As mentioned previously in Chapter 2, two vice-presidents and about fifteen key members of the Chinese Academy of Sciences

Table 3: Communist China's Estimated Foreign Trade in 1969
(in millions of U. S. dollars)

Countries	Chinese Exports	Chinese Imports	Countries	Chinese Exports	Chinese Imports
Hong Kong	326.0	1.0	Syria	17.0	17.0
Japan	234.0	390.0	Iraq	17.0	7.0
Singapore	140.0	59.0	Sweden	16.0	18.0
Britain	90.0	124.0	United Arab Republic	14.0	25.0
North Vietnam	90.0	20.0	Sudan	13.0	19.0
West Germany	84.0	151.0	Nigeria	13.0	0.7
Albania	75.0	35.0	Belgium	12.0	17.0
France	72.0	42.0	Morocco	12.0	7.0
Italy	64.0	56.0	Lebanon	12.0	unknown
Cuba	50.0	80.0	Libya	12.0	unknown
North Korea	50.0	50.0	Hungary	10.3	9.5
Ceylon	47.0	40.0	New Zealand	9.0	6.0
Australia	40.0	117.0	Austria	9.0	4.0
Rumania	40.0	42.0	Denmark	9.0	2.0
Czechoslovakia	33.0	28.0	Algeria	7.0	9.0
East Germany	29.0	31.0	Finland	6.0	6.0
Netherlands	28.0	24.0	Cambodia*	6.0	0.5
Pakistan	28.0	24.0	Norway	5.7	5.0
Soviet Union	27.0	28.0	Ghana	5.0	1.2
Kuwait	27.0	0.2	Senegal	5.0	unknown
Canada	25.0	114.0	Jordan	4.6	0.5
Switzerland	19.0	17.0	Tanzania	4.0	8.0
Poland	18.0	24.0	Peru	4.0	unknown

Table 3: Communist China's Estimated Foreign Trade in 1969 (Continued)

Countries	Chinese Exports	Chinese Imports	Countries	Chinese Exports	Chinese Imports
Outer Mongolia	3.5	1.0	Yugoslavia	1.0	1.0
Mauritania	3.0	unknown	Spain	1.0	0.8
South Yemen	2.7	unknown	Argentina	1.0	0.4
Ireland	2.5	0.1	Mali	0.8	0.4
Sierra Leone	2.3	unknown	Cameroon (East)	0.6	unknown
Iran	2.0	1.0	Tunisia	0.5	0.8
Ethiopia	2.0	0.8	Chad	0.4	unknown
Niger	2.0	unknown	Greece	0.4	unknown
Togo	2.0	unknown	Chile	0.3	0.4
Venezuela	1.7	unknown	Turkey	0.2	0.2
Bulgaria	1.5	1.5	Guyana	0.2	unknown
Somalia	1.4	unknown	Iceland	0.2	unknown
Burma	1.3	unknown	Uganda	0.1	0.2
Dahomey	1.3	unknown	Portugal	0.1	unknown
Kenya	1.0	1.0	Brazil	unknown	0.4

* Cambodia and Communist China suspended diplomatic and trade relations in 1970.

Source: The Editor, "China's Foreign Trade in 1969," *Current Scene*, October 7, 1970, pp. 10–18; Bernhard Grossman, "International Economic Relations of the People's Republic of China," *Asian Survey*, September 1970, pp. 789–802; George Ginsburgs and Arthur Stahnke, "Communist China's Trade Relations with Latin America," *Asian Survey*, September 1970, pp. 803–819; Patrick Yung, "Trade Ties Between Hong Kong and Mainland China," *Asian Survey*, September 1970, pp. 820–839; *The Los Angeles Times*, October 18, 1970, p. 3; and November 6, 1970, p. 5; *The Washington Post*, March 21, 1971, p. 22; and *The New York Times*, February 10, 1971, p. 9; and March 3, 1971, p. 14.

Table 4: Communist China's Estimated Foreign Trade Between 1966 and 1969 (in millions of U. S. dollars)

	1966	1967	1968	1969
Chinese Exports	2,170	1,915	1,890	2,060
Chinese Imports	2,035	1,945	1,820	1,825
Total Trade:	4,205	3,860	3,710	3,885
Trade with Non-Communist Countries	3,105	3,060	2,910	3,100
Trade with Communist Countries	1,100	800	800	785

Source: The Editor, "China's Foreign Trade in 1969," *Current Scene,* October 7, 1970, p. 2.

had been purged by June 1968. The Academy has been under military control since December 1967. Today members of the Academy are engaged in "self-education" and "self-examination" and intensively studying Maoism.[59] By opposing "Red" to "expert" and forcing the either/or choice between them, the Cultural Revolution has left deep scars within Communist China's small technocratic elite. (Communist China has stopped publication of nearly all scientific journals for the past five years). Undoubtedly, this has considerably impeded Communist China's progress in nuclear research and other areas of scientific and technological development for the past five years.

Peking's missile program was largely insulated from the upheavals of the Cultural Revolution, but the development of medium-range missiles has apparently slowed down.[60] (The State Council's Seventh Ministry of Machine Building is in charge of developing aircraft, rockets, missiles and other accessory electronic parts. It is believed that the Mao-Lin regime spends roughly $1 billion a year—ten to twelve per cent of Communist China's gross national product—on scientific research and development.)[61] Communist China had successfully launched its first man-made earth satellite in April 1970,[62] and its second one in March 1971.[63] These developments caused little surprise among Western intelligence experts. U. S. Defense Secretary Melvin Laird told Congress in February 1970 that the Chinese Communists would "attempt to test-launch their first ICBM or space booster in the near future." What did surprise these experts, however, was the fact that Peking took considerably longer than they estimated to put it up.

The educational system in most parts of Communist China remains chaotic. Primary and secondary schools have generally resumed classes in 1968 after being closed for two years starting from the spring of 1966 (when the student Red Guards emerged). But it has been only since the fall of 1970 that universities have begun enrolling students again, and these have been mainly in science and engineering schools.[64] Studies in the arts and humanities still appear to be paralyzed by the problems of the revision of teaching materials and of ideological reform.[65] As of this writing, normal academic life has apparently not resumed throughout the country, partly because of recent exile of millions of young ex-Red Guard students to the hinterlands for manual labor along with purged teachers and administrators, and partly because of Chairman Mao's new directives of "revolutionizing" education.[66]

The new "revolutionized" educational system shortens schooling periods, gives limited attention to conventional studies (i. e., liberal arts), and emphasizes manual labor, vocational training (that is to say, to work in factories and on farms), and political indoctrination.[67] Above all, great emphasis has been given to studying the Thought of Mao Tse-tung and to such political activity as "remoulding oneself" ideologically.[68]

Throughout the country, factories have assumed managerial and financial control of schools formerly run by municipal Party-government authorities. The management and financing of rural schools, also formerly run by Party-government bureaucracies in the main, have been taken over by collective farm units called production brigades (usually encompassing one to three villages) and communes. Under the current "revolutionized" Chinese Communist educational system, the twelve years formerly required to complete middle school is cut to nine years. Middle school graduates in the future must work on farms or in factories at least for a few years before becoming eligible for advanced training at a university. At the university, the required course is cut in half and schooling period is shortened from five to two or three years. As far as curriculum content is concerned, academic studies are almost eliminated in primary and secondary schools, leaving as basic arithmetic, physics, and agronomy. Military drill, practical techniques for farm and factories, and study of the Thought of Mao Tse-tung have become the main subjects.[69] Many former teachers are replaced by new, inexperienced, academically unqualified but politically acceptable teachers. Entrance examinations have been abolished, and new admission policies place more emphasis on class background.

Unrest and apathy are widespread among students still remaining at schools, for they are faced with the possibility that at any time they may be assigned to remote mountainous regions for hard labor. They react with bitter resentment to the managerial and financial take-over of their schools by peasants and workers, supported by soldiers, whom they despise as their intellectual inferiors who have too little book knowledge or "cannot even read a character when it is written big."

The excesses of the Cultural Revolution and the current "revolutionized" educational system have gone too far in putting politics in command in education. Mao's present "revolutionized" education may, in the words of the Editor of *Current Scene,* "change traditional Chinese attitudes which scorn manual labor and view education as an elitist passport to white collar officialdom,"[70] and also fill the Peking regime's short-run requirements for a politically trustworthy factory and peasantry work force equipped for tasks requiring simple skill. But it may leave a whole generation of Chinese youth ill-educated, and deprive the country's scientific and technological establishment of thousands of skilled university graduates, thereby denying them the tools of modernization.

Another important impact of the Cultural Revolution has been a fraying of Communist China's social fabric. In addition to political friction and lingering factionalism, Mao's Cultural Revolution has left a legacy of local (i. e., family and clan) animosities, feuds, and vendettas for "squaring blood debts" in many parts of the country, and this legacy has not yet been put aside. Undoubtedly, this result of the Cultural Revolution may continue to impede Peking's current efforts to restore order and stability.

Although a step toward resumption of normal government activity in Communist China was taken right after the Ninth Party Congress, the Chinese Communist government, over which the Party exercises control through an interlocking directorate, has not been fully reconstituted even at the top. Many cabinet members were purged from office during the height of the Cultural Revolution, and their ministries, if functioning at all, have been operating under officials of lesser rank. (Some twenty ministers of the forty were purged from their posts during the Cultural Revolution.)[71] At one stage, cabinet ministries were taken over by the military. To date, there has been no definite indication that the military control of the cabinet has been lifted. As of April 1971, there were many ministerial posts to fill, and the prospect was that many, if not most, would go to military men. The forthcoming Fourth National People's Congress will tell us how far the Chinese mainland has gone in restoring traditional lines of government authority.

By and large, with the Cultural Revolution now in its fifth year, Chairman Mao, who celebrated his seventy-seventh birthday a short while ago, is faced with a melancholy prospect: despite all his efforts to impose upon his country his militant dogma of "permanent revolution," the China of his sunset years is likely to be a pluralistic "revisionist" state.

Despite Mao's failure in the Cultural Revolution, there is neither danger nor signs of an imminent collapse of the Mao-Lin regime in Peking or the Chinese People's Republic. As long as the Chinese People's Liberation Army remains united, as long as Chairman Mao, supported by his constitutionally designated successor, "Marshal" Lin Piao, remains alive and alert, Communist China seems likely to hold together.

What the fiasco of the Cultural Revolution most vividly demonstrates is that the Thought of Mao Tse-tung is now very much dead as a source of national unity and as a force for progress in modernization. The major setbacks Mao suffered in both the Great Leap Forward and the Cultural Revolution have destroyed once and for all the credibility of Maoism as the sole "magic" formula for the future of Communist China.

Chairman Mao led the Chinese Communist revolution to ultimate triumph with indestructible iron will. He also unified the country—with its centuries-old centrifugal tendency—and laid the solid foundations of the new Communist order in his country in the early and mid-1950s. His great revolutionary achievements in the past, up to the advent of the Great Leap Forward of 1958, will undoubtedly make him one of the great men in Chinese history. But he wanted more—perhaps much more. He wanted to make his militant dogma an "immortal" guiding philosophy for the future of his country.

Chairman Mao remains a romantic Communist revolutionary whose ideas are rooted essentially in the past (the romantic Yenan guerrilla experience). As Communist China moves further toward modernization, the validity of his rigid dogmatism has been increasingly called into question and his ideas to promote China's greatness have not worked. He seeks modernization, but he opposes the requisites of modernization. This is the tragedy of Mao and his romantic revolutionary ideology: as Communist China changes, he may already be outliving his time.

Communist China is now concentrating on internal development, has recovered both from the economic disruptions and the disturbing uncertainties of the Cultural Revolution and wishes to resume its active role in international diplomacy. If the economic performance and the relative political stability of the country continue to improve in 1971, a period of sustained internal economic growth and political coherence will prevail. (It must be emphasized that the success in Peking's current drive for economic recovery and growth depends very much on avoiding armed hostilities with the Soviet Union, threatened by the territorial dispute.)

If this trend is thwarted by the factional power struggle, the weakened ruling political structure, the divided leadership, and by escalation of the Sino-Soviet boundary dispute into a direct military confrontation with Moscow, more upheavals and disintegration are likely to follow. The loyalty and discipline of the army will be the factors deciding whether the country will be able to preserve domestic tranquility and stability.

Mao Tse-tung appears to be nearing the end of his long and remarkable political career. An important question arises then as to what will happen in Communist China after Mao passes away. Much will depend on *when* the Party Chairman dies (and it must be emphasized that projecting the immediate future of China after Mao can be no more than educated speculation at best).

If Chairman Mao dies before Communist China achieves a sustained economic growth after recovering fully from the disruptions of the Cultural Revolution and the new power structure enthroned by the Ninth Party Congress of April 1969 in the form of Party-government rebuilding is stabilized and consolidated, there would be a greater likelihood of serious disunity possibly a breakup—in the Peking regime. Under the circumstances, the following three possibilities will get the most attention: (a) the disintegration of the country into regional "Red warlordism"; (b) the Communist-type military dictatorship under young Turk army officers; and (c) the takeover of the Mao-Lin regime by a coalition of the moderate civilian leaders like Premier Chou En-lai and the army, and the gradual abandonment of the Cultural Revolution.

If Chairman Mao lives until the new power framework settles in and the economy flourishes, a collective leadership will be likely to emerge after Mao's death, as happened in the Soviet Union after Stalin's death. Vice-Chairman and "Marshal" Lin Piao will preside over any post-Mao collective leadership (granting that he outlives his mentor). The sources of Mr. Lin's power lie primarily in his endorsement by Mao as his "close comrade-in-arms" and in his hold over the army as Defense Minister and one of its most brilliant commanders. He will not, however, dominate the post-Mao collective leadership in Mao's fashion. He is not in good health, and lacks Mao's unquestioned prestige and charisma. With Mao gone, he might be vulnerable to challenge by dissident Party or military factions.

Under Lin Piao, the various factional groups which emerged during the Cultural Revolution will operate. (Lin Piao's rule may not last long, for his is, at sixty-three, a frail, sickly man plagued by chronic tuberculosis and serious wounds from the Korean War.) Undoubtedly, the army will be the dominant faction and have a strong voice in the post-Mao collective leadership. (A putsch by some ambitious military officers or group cannot be ruled out.) The post-Mao regime, because of its factional cleavage, will not be strong at the center, and the country's provincial power, mostly under military domination, will probably continue to grow, increasing the process of decentralization.

Of course, one cannot entirely preclude the possibility that the differences which split the post-Mao regime will be so wide and fundamental that the post-Mao collective leadership may fail and face a period of turmoil and bloodshed, with the rapid rise and fall of top elite members.

Within this speculative milieu, one of the first and most obvious developments after Mao's death may be the political demise of Mao's radical palace coterie, led by Chiang Ching, which has so far been able to exist only on the strength of Chairman Mao's personal prestige and favor.

The most important and fundamental question, however, is not who, but what will survive Mao: the most relevant question is whether Mao's romantic revolutionary fundamentalism and his grand design for Communist China will survive his death. Since the credibility of Mao's militant dogmatism has already suffered both in the Great Leap Forward and in the Cultural Revolution, it is unlikely that Maoism or the Thought of Mao Tse-tung as a guiding political philosophy will long survive the death of its creator.

NOTES TO CHAPTER 5

1. *The Los Angeles Times*, August 14, 1970, p. 7 (Part II).

2. *Sing Tao Jih Pao*, Hong Kong, February 11, 1971.

3. *Ming Pao Evening News*, Hong Kong, February 23, 1971.

4. *Peking Review*, August 6, 1969, pp. 7–8.

5. Mao Tse-tung, *Selected Works* (New York: International Publishers, 1935), Vol. 1, p. 75.

6. *Ibid.*

7. *Peking Review*, April 30, 1969, p. 25.

8. On August 16, 1969, *Jen-min Jih-pao*, the Maoist party newspaper, admitted this fact openly.

9. For Peking's admission of the continuing factional strife among the Maoist "rebels," see *Jen-min Jih-pao*, June 9 and October 21, 1969; *Hung Ch'i*, August 25, 1969; and *Chieh fang chün Pao*, August 25, 1969.

10. Peking's first appeal for national unity in the face of a possible Soviet military attack was made on June 9, 1969. *Jen-min Jih-pao*, June 9, 1969; and *Chieh-fang-chün Pao*, June 9, 1969.

11. *The New York Times*, August 6, 1970, p. 3.

12. *Ibid.*

13. *Ibid.*

14. *Ibid.*

15. *Ibid.*

16. *The New York Times*, December 26, 1969, p. 3.

17. See Parris H. Chang, "The Revolutionary Committee in China; Two Case Studies: Heilungkiang and Honan," *Current Scene*, June 1, 1968, pp. 1–20; The Editor, "Revolutionary Committee Leadership— China's Current Provincial Authorities," *Current Scene*, October 18, 1968, pp. 1–28; The Editor, "China's Revolutionary Committees," *Current*

Scene, December 6, 1968, pp. 1–15; Richard Baum, "China: Year of the Mangoes," *Asian Survey,* January 1969, pp. 5–9; The Editor, "The Revolutionary Committee and the Party in the Aftermath of the Cultural Revolution," *Current Scene,* April 15, 1970, p. 2; and *The New York Times,* June 14, 1970, p. 8.

18. *Ibid.*

19. *New China News Agency,* May 21, 1970; *Shantung Radio,* May 21, 1970; and *What's Happening on Mainland China,* August 9, 1970, pp. 2–4.

20. *Ibid.*

21. See footnote 17.

22. *Ibid.*

23. *Jen-min Jih-pao,* July 1, 1969; October 12, 1969; and January 1, 1970; *Hung Ch'i,* July 1, 1969; and *New China News Agency,* December 12, 1969.

24. *Jen-min Jih-pao,* July 4, 1970; and *New China News Agency,* July 11, 1970.

25. *What's Happening on Mainland China,* July 12, 1970, p. 3.

26. *Ibid.*

27. *Ibid.*

28. *Ibid.* See also *The New York Times,* March 21, 1971, p. 9.

29. Harry Harding, "China: Toward Revolutionary Pragmatism," *Asian Survey,* January 1971, p. 55; and *Current Scene,* October 7, 1970, p. 20.

30. *Jen-min Jih-pao,* July 1, 1969; and *Hung Ch'i,* July 1, 1969.

31. *Ibid.* See also *Jen-min Jih-pao,* October 1, 1969; and January 1, 1970; *New China News Agency,* December 17, 1969; and *Peking Review,* January 2, 1971, pp. 5–7.

32. *The Washington Post,* February 20, 1971, p. 13.

33. See *Appendix III.*

34. Mr. Tillman Durdin's dispatch from Hong Kong, in *The New York Times,* August 29, 1971, p. 18. See also Appendix III.

35. See Appendices II and III.

36. See, for example, *Jen-min Jih-pao,* October 4, 1969.

37. *The* (Baltimore) *Sun,* December 27, 1970, p. 6.

38. *Current Scene,* October 7, 1970, pp. 21–22; *Jen-min Jih-pao,* July 1, 1970; and *Chieh-fang-chün Pao,* July 1, 1970.

39. See, for example, *Jen-min Jih-pao,* January 21, 1970; and *Radio Canton,* April 1, 1970.

40. See, for example, *Jen-min Jih-pao,* November 2, 1969.

41. See, for example, *The New York Times,* February 28, 1971, p. 6.

42. *Peking Review,* February 13, 1970, pp. 3–9, 20.

43. See *The New York Times,* June 7, 1970, p. 12; *The Washington Post,* June 4, 1960, p. 21; and Richard Hughes, "Mao Makes the Trials Run on Time," *The New York Times Sunday Magazine,* August 23, 1970, pp. 23, 67–68.

44. *The New York Times,* June 18, 1970, p. 8.

45. See *Current Scene,* July 17, 1968, pp. 1–14; and May 3, 1969, pp. 1–14; *The New York Times,* January 17, 1969, p. 64; May 19, 1969, p. 10; Robert F. Dernberger, "Economic Realities and China's Political Economics," *Bulletin of the Atomic Scientists,* February 1969, pp. 34–38; and Jan S. Prybyla, "Communist China: The Economy and the Revolution," *Current History,* September 1968, pp. 135–137.

46. *Peking Review,* September 25, 1970, pp. 7–10; Colina MacDougal, "The Struggle to Come," *Far Eastern Economic Review,* June 4, 1970, pp. 59–61; Ilsa Sharp, "A Hope or a Leap?" *Far Eastern Economic Review,* June 4, 1970, pp. 12–13; and L. F. Goodstadt, "Farm vs. Factory," *Far Eastern Economic Review,* June 18, 1970, pp. 12–13.

47. *The New York Times,* January 18, 1971, p. 46 (Economic Survey of Asia and the Pacific); March 11, 1971, p. 3; and Harry Harding, "China: Toward Revolutionary Pragmatism," *Asian Survey,* January 1971, p. 60.

48. *Ibid.*

49. See footnote 45. See also *The New York Times,* November 19, 1969, p. 10, January 19, 1970, pp. 1 and 58 (special yearly economic review on Asia); and June 7, 1970, p. 14; *The Washington Post,* June 9, 1970, p. 14; and *The* (Baltimore) *Sun,* April 10, 1970, p. 4.

50. *The New York Times,* January 18, 1971, p. 46 (Economic Survey of Asia and the Pacific).

51. *The New York Times,* November 17, 1970, p. 6; and March 11, 1971, p. 3.

52. See footnote 49.

53. *Ibid.*

54. *The New York Times,* October 4, 1970, p. 9; and March 11, 1971, p. 3; and *The Washington Post,* March 21, 1971, p. 4 (K).

55. *Peking Review,* January 8, 1971, pp. 6–8; and *The New York Times,* January 18, 1971, p. 46 (Economic Survey of Asia and the Pacific).

56. *Ibid.*

57. *Jen-min Jih-pao,* October 1, 1970; *Peking Review,* January 1, 1971, pp. 8–10; and *Current Scene,* November 7, 1970, pp. 19–20.

58. *Ibid.*

59. See *The Washington Post,* May 3, 1970, p. 4 (Sunday Outlook Section).

60. *The* (London) *Economist,* September 20, 1969, p. 36.

61. *The Washington Post,* May 3, 1970, p. 4 (Sunday Outlook Section).

62. *Peking Review,* April 30, 1970, pp. 4–13.

63. *Peking Review,* March 19, 1971, p. 17; and *New China News Agency,* March 16, 1971.

64. *The Washington Post,* October 1, 1970, p. 17; and December 12, 1970, p. 23; and *The New York Times,* September 25, 1970, p. 10.

65. *Ibid.*

66. *Current Scene,* January 7, 1971, pp. 16–18.

67. See *Jen-min Jih-pao,* April 21, 1969; and May 12, 1969; *New China News Agency,* April 18, 1969; The Editor, "Educational Reform in Rural China," *Current Scene,* February 8, 1969, pp. 1–17; The Editor, "Educational Reform and Rural Resettlement in Communist China," *Current Scene,* November 7, 1970, p. 1; *What's Happening on the Chinese Mainland,* March 23, 1969, pp. 1–4; *The New York Times,* December 12, 1968, p. 14; *The Los Angeles Times,* April 19, 1970, pp. 4–5 (Sunday Section D); *Peking Review,* August 2, 1968, p. 3; March 20, 1970, pp. 9–14, 24; and July 31, 1970, pp. 5–15; Donald J. Munro, "Marxism and Realities in China's Educational Policy: The Half-Work, Half-Study Model," *Asian Survey,* April 1967, pp. 254–272; and Gordon A. Bennett, "China's Continuing Revolution: Will It Be Permanent?" *Asian Survey,* January 1970, pp. 11–12.

68. *Ibid.*

69. *Ibid.*

70. Quoted from The Editor, "Educational Reform and Rural Resettlement in Communist China," *Current Scene,* November 7, 1970, p. 7.

71. *The New York Times,* October 26, 1970, p. 6; and December 27, 1970, p. 8.

APPENDICES

APPENDIX I

The Ninth Central Committee of the Chinese Communist Party†

(as of August 1971)

Abbreviations:

CC — Central Committee
CCP — Chinese Communist Party
NPC — National People's Congress
PLA — People's Liberation Army

Symbols:

*** member of Standing Committee, Politburo
** full member of Politburo
* alternate member of Politburo
++ was member of 8th Central Committee
+ was alternate member of 8th Central Committee

170 Full Members

MAO Tse-tung	(***; ++)	Chairman of CCP.
LIN Piao	(***; ++)	Vice-Chairman of CCP; Defense Minister.
CHANG Chih-ming	(military; Lin Piao clique)	President of the PLA Rear Service School, Peking; Political Commissar of PLA Logistics Department; Deputy Leader of the Cultural Revolution Group under the CCP CC.
CHANG Chun-chiao	(**; military; Chiang Ching clique)	Chairman of Shanghai Municipal Revolutionary Committee; First Political Commissar of Nanking Military Region; Deputy Leader of the Cultural Revolution Group under the CCP CC.
CHANG Fu-heng		

† Compiled on the basis of information obtained from various official Chinese Communist media sources, Chinese Nationalist materials, and Hong Kong publications.

CHANG Fu-kuei	(peasant)	Member of Shantung Provincial Revolutionary Committee; an agricultural labor model.
CHANG Heng-yun	(peasant)	Peasant from Shensi Province.
CHANG Kuo-hua	(military; Lin Piao clique)	Chairman of Szechuan Provincial Revolutionary Committee; Commander and First Political Commissar of Chengtu Military District; former Area Military Commander and Party Chief in Tibet.
CHANG Ta-chih	(+; military)	Deputy Chairman of Kansu Provincial Revolutionary Committee; Commander of Lanchow Military Region.
CHANG Ti-hsueh	(administrative cadre, Chou En-lai clique)	Deputy Chairman of Hupeh Provincial Revolutionary Committee; formerly Second Secretary of Party Provincial Committee and Governor of Hupeh.
CHANG Tien-yun	(military)	Deputy Director of PLA Logistics Department.
CHANG Ting-cheng	(++; administrative cadre)	Chief Procurator of Supreme People's Procuratorate.
CHANG Tsai-chien	(military)	Deputy Political Commissar of Nanking Military Region.
CHANG Yi-hsiang	(military)	Commander of PLA railway troops.
CHANG Yun-yi	(++; military, Chou En-lai clique)	Member of National Defense Council; formerly Second Secretary of Control Commission, CC CCP.

CHEN Chi-han	(administrative cadre)	Member of National Defense Council; Vice President of Supreme People's Court; formerly member of Control Commission, CC CCP.
CHEN Hsi-lien	(**; +; military)	Chairman of Liaoning Provincial Revolutionary Committee; Commander of Shenyang Military Region.
CHEN Hsien-jui	(military)	Deputy Political Commissar of Peking Military Region; Member of Chinese People's Political Consultative Conference.
CHEN Kang	(military)	Deputy Chairman of Yunnan Provincial Revolutionary Committee; Deputy Commander of Kuming Military Region.
CHEN Po-ta (in disgrace?)	(***; ++; Party cadre, Mao clique)	Head of Cultural Revolution Group under CC CCP; formerly Mao Tse-tung's political secretary and ghostwriter.
CHEN Shih-chu	(military, Lin Piao clique)	Commander of PLA Engineer Corps.
CHEN YI	(++; ex-military)	Vice Premier; Foreign Minister (retired recently); Vice Chairman of Military Commission of 9th CC CCP.
CHEN Yu	(++; administrative cadre; formerly Liu Shao-chi/Teng Hsiao-ping clique)	Deputy Chairman of Kwangtung Provincial Revolutionary Committee; formerly Secretary of Secretariat of Provincial Party Committee and Governor of Kwangtung.
CHEN Yun	(++; administrative cadre)	Vice Premier; an economist (who opposed Mao's radical Great Leap Forward Movement of 1958).

CHEN Yung-kuei (Party cadre, Mao clique) — Deputy Chairman of Shansi Provincial Revolutionary Committee; a national labor model; Party Secretary at Tachai Brigade, Hsiyang Hsien, Shansi.

CHENG Shih-ching (military, Lin Piao clique) — Chairman of Kiangsi Provincial Revolutionary Committee; Vice Political Commissar of Foochow Military Region; First Political Commissar of Kiangsi Military District.

CHENG Wei-shan (military) — Deputy Chairman of Peking Municipal Revolutionary Committee; Commander of Peking Military Region.

CHIANG Ching (female) (**; Mme. Mao Tse-tung) — First Deputy Head of the Cultural Revolution Group under CC CCP; a "cultural adviser" to PLA.

CHIANG Hsieh-yuan (military, Lin Piao clique) — Deputy Chief of Staff of Canton Military Region.

CHIANG Li-yin (female) (worker, Chiang Ching clique) — Railroad worker from Foochow, Fukien Province.

CHIANG Yung-hui (military, Lin Piao clique) — Chief of Staff of Shenyang Military Region.

CHIEN Chih-kuang (administrative cadre) — Vice Minister of Textile Industry.

CHI Teng-kuei (*; Party cadre) — Deputy Chairman of Honan Provincial Revolutionary Committee

CHIU Chuang-cheng (military) — Minister of 5th Ministry of Machine Building; Political Commissar of PLA Artillery Force; member of National Defense Council.

CHIU Hui-tso	(**; military, Lin Piao clique)	Deputy Chief of Staff; Director of PLA's General Rear Service Department; Deputy Head of PLA Cultural Revolution Group.
CHIU Kuo-kuang	(military)	Deputy Chairman of Kwangtung Provincial Revolutionary Committee; Deputy Commander of Canton Military Region.
CHOU Chien-jen	(administrative cadre)	Deputy Chairman of Chekiang Provincial Revolutionary Committee; formerly non-Communist Governor of Chekiang Province.
CHOU Chih-ping	(military)	Vice Minister of Metallurgical Industry.
CHOU En-lai	(**; +-;)	Premier.
CHOU Hsing	(military)	Acting Chairman of Yunnan Provincial Revolutionary Committee; Political Commissar of Yunnan Military District; formerly Governor of Yunnan Province and Deputy Minister of Public Security in Peking.
CHU Teh	(**; ++; ex-military)	PLA ex-Marshal; President of National People's Congress.
FAN Wen-lan	(+; Party cadre)	Historian; Member of Standing Committee of National People's Congress.
HAN Hsien-chu	(+; military, Lin Piao clique)	Chairman of Fukien Provincial Revolutionary Committee; Commander of Foochow Military Region; Deputy Chief of General Staff of PLA; Member of National Defense Council.

HSIA Pang-yin — Member of Standing Committee of Hupeh Provincial Revolutionary Committee; "responsible person" of Wuhan Workers Congress.

HSIAO Ching-kuang (++; military, Lin Piao clique) — Deputy Defense Minister; Commander of PLA Navy; Member of National Defense Council.

HSIEH Chia-hsiang (military) — Deputy Political Commissar of Chengtu Military Region.

HSIEH Fu-chih (**; ++; military, Mao clique) — Chairman of Peking Municipal Revolutionary Committee; First Political Commissar of Peking Military Region; Minister of Public Security (secret police); Vice Premier.

HSIEH Hsueh-kung (administrative cadre) — Chairman of Tientsin Municipal Revolutionary Committee; formerly First Party Secretary of Tientsin and Secretary of CCP North China Bureau.

HSIEN Heng-han (military) — Chairman of Kansu Provincial Revolutionary Committee; Political Commissar of Lanchow Military Region.

HSU Ching-hsien (administrative cadre) — Member of Standing Committee of Shanghai Municipal Revolutionary Committee.

HSU Hai-tung (++; ex-military) — Member of National Defense Council.

HSU Hsiang-chien (++; military, Chiang Ching clique) — Vice Chairman of National Defense Council; Head of PLA Cultural Revolution Group; Vice Chairman of Military Commission of 9th CC CCP.

HSU Shih-yu	(**; +; military, Lin Piao clique)	Deputy Defense Minister; Chairman of Kiangsu Provincial Revolutionary Committee; Commander of Nanking Military Region.
HU Chi-tsung	(administrative cadre)	Deputy Chairman of Kansu Provincial Revolutionary Committee; formerly Deputy Governor and acting First Party Secretary of Kansu.
HUA Kuo-feng	(administrative cadre)	Acting Chairman of Hunan Provincial Revolutionary Committee; formerly Deputy Governor of Hunan and a member of Hunan Party Secretariat.
HUANG Chen	(administrative cadre)	Ambassador to France.
HUANG Yung-sheng	(**; +; military, Lin Piao clique)	Chief of General Staff, PLA; Member of National Defense Council; Secretary-General and Member of Standing Committee of CCP Military Affairs Committee.
JAO Hsing-li	(peasant)	Deputy Chairman of Hupeh Provincial Revolutionary Committee; a national model peasant; Vice Chairman of Hupeh Provincial Association of Poor and Lower-Middle Peasants.
JEN Ssu-chung	(military)	Member of Kwangtung Provincial Revolutionary Committee; Deputy Political Commissar of Canton Military Region.
KANG Sheng	(***; ++; Party Cadre, Chiang Ching clique)	Adviser to Cultural Revolution Group under CC CCP.

KAO Wei-sung	(military)	Deputy Commander of Lanchow Military Region.
KENG Piao	(administrative cadre; ex-military)	Ambassador to Albania.
KUANG Jen-nung	(military)	Deputy Commander of PLA Air Force; Director of Civil Aviation Bureau.
KUNG Shih-chuan	(military, Lin Piao clique)	First Deputy Chairman of Kwangtung Provincial Revolutionary Committee; Political Commissar of Canton Military Region.
KUO Mo-jo	(administrative cadre)	Vice Chairman of National People's Congress; Member of Chinese Academy of Sciences; writer.
LAI Chi-fa	(administrative cadre)	Minister of Building Material Industry.
LI Chen	(administrative cadre; ex-military)	Responsible person of an administrative organization in Peking; formerly an officer in Shenyang Military Region.
LI Chiang	(administrative cadre)	Vice Minister of Foreign Trade.
LI Fu-chun	(++; administrative and Party cadre, Chou En-lai clique)	Vice Premier; Chairman of State Planning Commission.
LI Hsien-nien	(**; ++; ex-military)	Vice Premier; Minister of Finance.
LI Hsueh-feng	(*; ++; Party cadre, formerly Liu Shao-ch'i/Teng Hsiao-p'ing clique)	Former Chairman of Hopei Provincial Revolutionary Committee; First Secretary of North China Bureau of CC CCP and of Peking Municipal Party Committee.

LI Jui-shan	(administrative cadre)	Chairman of Shensi Provincial Revolutionary Committee; formerly Secretary of Secretariat of Provincial Party Committee and First Secretary of Changsha Municipal Party Committee.
LI Shui-ching	(military)	Chief of Staff of Tsinan Military Region.
LI Shun-ta	(peasant)	Member of Shansi Provincial Revolutionary Committee.
LI Ssu-kuang (dead)	(scientist)	Minister of Geology; Vice Chairman of National Committee of Chinese Political Consultative Conference.
LI Su-wen (female)	(merchant)	Sales clerk at Shenyang Food Company.
LI Ta-chang	(+; administrative and Party cadre)	Deputy Chairman of Szechuan Provincial Revolutionary Committee; formerly Governor and Party Secretary of Szechuan and Secretary of CCP Southwest Bureau.
LI Teh-sheng	(*; military)	Director of PLA's General Political Department; Chairman of Anhwei Provincial Revolutionary Committee; Commander of Anhwei Military District.
LI Tien-yu	(military, Lin Piao clique)	Deputy Chief of General Staff, PLA; Member of National Defense Council.
LI Tso-peng	(*?; military, Lin Piao clique)	Vice Commander and First Political Commissar of PLA Navy; Deputy Head of PLA Cultural Revolution Group; Member of National Defense Council.

LIANG Hsing-chu	(military, Lin Piao clique)	Deputy Chairman of Szechuan Provincial Revolutionary Committee; Commander of Chengtu Military Region.
LIU Chieh-ting	(military)	Deputy Chairman of Szechuan Provincial Revolutionary Committee; Deputy Political Commissar of Chengtu Military Region.
LIU Chien-hsun	(+; military, Lin Piao clique)	Chairman of Honan Provincial Revolutionary Committee; concurrently Political Commissar of Wuhan Military Region and First Political Commissar of Honan Military District; formerly First Party Secretary of Honan Province.
LIU Chun-yi	(administrative cadre)	Member of Standing Committee of Kwangtung Provincial Revolutionary Committee.
LIU Feng	(military)	Deputy Chairman of Hupeh Provincial Revolutionary Committee; Political Commissar of Wuhan Military Region.
LIU Hsi-chang	(worker)	Member of Standing Committee of Peking Municipal Revolutionary Committee.
LIU Hsien-chuan	(military, Lin Piao clique)	Chairman of Tsinghai Provincial Revolutionary Committee; Deputy Commander of Lanchow Military Region.
LIU Hsing-yuan	(military, Lin Piao clique)	Chairman of Kwangtung Provincial Revolutionary Committee; Deputy Political Commissar of Canton Military Region.

LIU Ke-ping
(in disgrace)

(+ +; military)

Former Chairman of Shansi Provincial Revolutionary Committee; First Political Commissar of both Peking Military Region and Shansi Military District; formerly Vice Governor of Shansi.

LIU Po-cheng

(**; ++; ex-military)

Deputy Chairman of National Defense Council; Vice Chairman of National People's Congress.

LIU Sheng-tien

(administrative cadre)

Deputy Chairman of Liaoning Provincial Revolutionary Committee; a "responsible person" of Liaoning Peasants Congress.

LIU Tzu-hou

(—; administrative cadre)

Acting Chairman of Hopeh Provincial Revolutionary Committee; formerly Governor of Hopeh and Secretary of CCP North China Bureau.

LIU Wei

(administrative cadre)

Deputy Minister of 2nd Machine Industry.

LU Jui-lin

(military)

Deputy Chairman of Yunnan Provincial Revolutionary Committee; Deputy Commander of Kunming Military Region.

LU Tien-chi

LU Yu-lan (female)

(Party cadre, Chiang Ching clique)

Member of Standing Committee of Hopei Provincial Revolutionary Committee; Secretary of Party branch at Linhsinhsiapao Commune.

LUNG Shu-chin

(military, Lin Piao clique)

Chairman of Sinkiang Autonomous Region Revolutionary Committee; Commander of Sinkiang Military Region.

MA Fu-chuan (military, Chiang Ching clique) A PLA soldier.

MO Hsien-yao (peasant) Member of Standing Committee of Chekiang Provincial Revolutionary Committee.

NAN Ping (military) Chairman of Chekiang Provincial Revolutionary Committee; Political Commissar of Chekiang Military District.

NIEH Jung-chen (++; Party-administrative cadre; ex-military) Vice Premier; Chairman of State Science and Technology Commission; Deputy Chairman of National Defense Council; Vice Chairman of Military Commission of 9th CC CCP.

NI Chih-fu

NIEN Chi-jung Deputy Chairman of Kansu Provincial Revolutionary Committee; a militia squad leader.

PAN Fu-sheng (in disgrace) (+; military) Former Chairman of Heilungkiang Provincial Revolutionary Committee; Political Commissar of Shenyang Military Region and Heilungkiang Military District.

PAN Shih-kao

PAOJIHLETAI (female) (a poor herdswoman) Chairman of Wushenchao Commune Revolutionary Committee of Inner Mongolia.

PENG Shao-hui (military) Deputy Chief of Staff, PLA.

PI Ting-chun (military) Deputy Chairman of Fukien Provincial Revolutionary Committee; Deputy Commander of Foochow Military Region.

SAIFUDIN	(+; military)	Deputy Chairman of Sinkiang Autonomous Region Revolutionary Committee; Deputy Commander of Sinkiang Military Region.
SHEN Mao-kung	(worker)	Member of Standing Committee of Honan Provincial Revolutionary Committee; Head of Chengchow Workers' Congress.
SU Ching	(military)	A "responsible person" of a department at the national defense industry.
SU Yu	(−+; military)	Deputy Minister of Defense.
TAN Fu-jen (died)	(military, Lin Piao clique)	Former Chairman of Yunnan Provincial Revolutionary Committee; Political Commissar of Kunming Military Region.
TANG Chi-shan	(worker)	Member of Standing Committee of Honan Provincial Revolutionary Committee.
TANG Chung-fu	(worker)	Member of Standing Committee of Hunan Provincial Revolutionary Committee.
TENG Hai-ching (in disgrace)	(military)	Formerly Chairman of Inner Mongolia Autonomous Region Revolutionary Committee; Vice Commander of Peking Military Region; Commander of Inner Mongolia Military Region.
TENG Tai-yuan	(++; administrative cadre)	Former Minister of Railway.
TENG Tzu-hui	(++; administrative cadre)	Deputy Director of State Planning Commission; Vice Chairman of Chinese People's Political Consultative Conference.

TENG Ying-chao (female)	(++; Mme. Chou En-lai)	Vice Chairman of All-China Federation of Women.
TIEN Hua-kuei	(Party cadre)	Member of Standing Committee of Kwangtung Provincial Revolutionary Committee.
TIEN Pao	(+; administrative cadre)	Deputy Chairman of Szechuan Provincial Revolutionary Committee; formerly known as Sung-chiehyuehhsi, when serving as Deputy Governor of Szechuan.
TING Sheng	(military, Lin Piao clique)	Deputy Commander of Canton Military Region.
TSAI Chang (female)	(++; Mme. Li Fu-chun)	Chairman of All-China Federation of Women.
TSAI Hsieh-pin	(peasant)	Member of Standing Committee of Szechuan Provincial Revolutionary Committee.
TSAI Shu-mei (female)		Member of Standing Committee of Tientsin Municipal Revolutionary Committee.
TSAO Li-huai	(military)	Deputy Commander of PLA Air Force.
TSAO Yi-ou (female)	(Mme. Kang Sheng)	Formerly Deputy Director of Organization Department of CCP North China Bureau.
TSENG Kuo-hua	(military)	Deputy Commander of PLA Air Force.
TSENG Shan	(++; administrative cadre)	Minister of Internal Affairs.
TSENG Shao-shan	(military)	Deputy Chairman of Liaoning Provincial Revolutionary Committee; Political Commissar of Shenyang Military Region.

TSENG Ssu-yu	(military, Lin Piao clique)	Chairman of Hupeh Provincial Revolutionary Committee; Commander of Wuhan Military Region.
TSUNG Hsi-yun	(worker)	Member of Kirin Provincial Revolutionary Committee.
TU Ping	(military, Lin Piao clique)	Member of Standing Committee of Kiangsu Provincial Revolutionary Committee; Second Political Commissar of Nanking Military Region.
TUNG Ming-hui	(worker)	Worker from Wuhan Iron and Steel Corporation in Hupeh Province.
TUNG Pi-wu	(**; ++)	Vice Chairman of Chinese People's Republic.
WANG Chao-chu	(worker, Chiang Ching clique)	A worker on Nanking Railway Bridge.
WANG Chen	(++; administrative cadre; ex-military)	Minister of Agricultural Reclamation.
WANG Chin-hsi (died)	(worker, Chiang Ching clique)	Deputy Chairman of Taching Oilfields Revolutionary Committee; a national labor model.
WANG Hsiao-yu (purged)	(military, Chiang Ching clique)	Former Chairman of Shantung Provincial Revolutionary Committee; Former First Political Commissar of Tsinan Military Region; formerly Deputy Mayor of Tsiengtao.
WANG Hsin-ting	(military)	Deputy Chief of Staff, PLA; Deputy Leader of PLA Cultural Revolution Group.

WANG Hsiu-chen (female)	(worker, Chiang Ching clique)	Chairman of a Shanghai textile factory revolutionary committee; Member of Standing Committee of Shanghai Municipal Revolutionary Committee.
WANG Huai-hsiang	(military)	Chairman of Kirin Provincial Revolutionary Committee; Political Commissar of Kirin Military District.
WANG Hui-chiu	(military)	Deputy Political Commissar of PLA Air Force.
WANG Hung-kun	(military, Lin Piao clique)	Admiral and Vice Commander of PLA Navy; Member of National Defense Council.
WANG Hung-wen	(worker, Chiang Ching clique)	Deputy Chairman of Shanghai Municipal Revolutionary Committee; "responsible person" of Shanghai Workers' Headquarters.
WANG Kuo-fan	(peasant)	Member of Standing Committee of Hopei Provincial Revolutionary Committee; a national model peasant.
WANG Pai-tan		
WANG Ping-chang	(military, Lin Piao clique)	Minister of 7th Machine Industry; Deputy Commander of PLA Air Force.
WANG Shou-tao	(++; Party cadre)	Deputy Chairman of Kwangtung Provincial Revolutionary Committee; formerly Secretary of CCP Central-South Bureau.
WANG Shu-sheng	(++; military)	Deputy Minister of Defense; Member of National Defense Council.

WEI Feng-ying (female)	(worker, Chiang Ching clique)	Deputy Chairman of Liaoning Provincial Revolutionary Committee; a "model worker" representative of pro-Mao mass organization.
WEI Kuo-ching	(+; military)	Chairman of Kwangsi Provincial Revolutionary Committee; First Political Commissar of Kwangsi Military District; formerly First Secretary of Kwangsi Party Committee.
WEI Ping-kuei	(worker, Chiang Ching clique)	Deputy Chairman of Liaoning Provincial Revolutionary Committee.
WEN Yu-cheng	(military, Lin Piao clique)	Deputy Chief of Staff, PLA; Commander of Peking Garrison.
WU Fa-hsien	(**; military, Lin Piao clique)	Commander of PLA Air Force.
WU Jui-lin	(military)	Deputy Commander of PLA Navy.
WU Kuei-hsien (female)	(worker, Chiang Ching clique)	Member of Shensi Provincial Revolutionary Committee; a textile worker.
WU Ta-sheng	(military)	Deputy Chairman of Kiangsu Provincial Revolutionary Committee; leading officer of a unit under the Nanking Military Region.
WU Tao	(military, Lin Piao clique)	Deputy Chairman of Inner Mongolia Autonomous Region Revolutionary Committee; Political Commissar of Inner Mongolia Military Region.
WU Teh	(++; military)	Deputy Chairman of Peking Municipal Revolutionary Committee; Political Commissar of Peking Garrison.

YANG Chun-fu　(Party cadre)　Deputy Chairman of Liaoning Provincial Revolutionary Committee; formerly Party Secretary of Liaoning and First Secretary of Shenyang Party Committee.

YANG Fu-chen (female)　(worker, Chiang Ching clique)　Worker at Shanghai textile factory.

YANG Teh-chih　(+; military, Lin Piao clique)　Chairman of Shantung Provincial Revolutionary Committee; Commander of Tsinan Military Region.

YAO Wen-yuan　(**; administrative cadre, Chiang Ching clique)　Deputy Chairman of Shanghai Municipal Revolutionary Committee; Member of Cultural Revolution Group under CC CCP; formerly Editor-in-Chief of Shanghai *Liberation Daily.*

YEH Chien-ying　(**; ++; ex-military, Lin Piao clique)　Deputy Chairman of National Defense Council; an old PLA Marshal.

YEN Chun (female)　(**; Mme. Lin Piao)　Vice Chairman Lin Piao's personal secretary; Member of PLA Cultural Revolution Group.

YU Chiu-li　(administrative cadre; ex-military)　Minister of Petroleum.

YU Sang　(administrative cadre; ex-military)　Deputy Minister of Public Security.

YUAN Sheng-ping　(military, Lin Piao clique)　Member of Standing Committee of Shantung Provincial Revolutionary Committee; Second Political Commissar of Tsinan Military Region.

109 Alternate Members

CHANG Chi-hui　(military)　Commander of 1st Division of PLA Air Force.

CHANG Chiang-lin (military, Lin Piao clique) First Vice-Chairman of Tsinghai Provincial Revolutionary Committee; Deputy Commander of Tsinghai Military District.

CHANG Hsi-ting (female) (administrative cadre) Deputy Chairman of Szechuan Provincial Revolutionary Committee; formerly Secretary of Pin Municipal Party Committee.

CHANG Hsiu-chuan (military) Director of Political Department of PLA Navy; Member of PLA Cultural Revolution Group.

CHANG Jih-ching (purged) (military, Lin Piao clique) Formerly Deputy Chairman of Shansi Provincial Revolutionary Committee; Political Commissar of Peking Military Region and Second Political Commissar of Shansi Military District.

CHANG Ling-pin (military) Deputy Director of PLA Logistics Department.

CHANG Shih-chung

CHANG Ssu-chou (peasant) Deputy Chairman of Szechuan Provincial Revolutionary Committee; agricultural labor hero.

CHANG Yen-cheng

CHANG Ying-tsai (military) Deputy Commander of PLA 13th Army; battle hero.

CHAO Chi-min (military) Deputy Commander of PLA Navy.

CHAO Feng

CHAO Hsing-yuan (military) Deputy Commander of PLA 40th Army.

CHEN Ho-fa

CHEN Hua-tang (administrative cadre; ex-military)

Vice Chairman of National Defense Scientific Committee; formerly Deputy Air Force Commander at Foochow Military Region.

CHEN Jen-chi (military)

Political Commissar of PLA Artillery Force.

CHEN Kan-feng (Red Guard)

Member of Standing Committee of Shanghai Municipal Revolutionary Committee; "responsible person" of Shanghai Red Guard Congress.

CHEN Li-yun (military)

First Deputy Chairman of Chekiang Provincial Revolutionary Committee; concurrently Deputy Political Commissar of Chekiang Military District and a "responsible person" of PLA Air Force units in Chekiang area.

CHENG San-sheng (military, Lin Piao clique)

Deputy Chairman of Tientsin Municipal Revolutionary Committee; Commander of Tientsin Garrison.

CHIANG Pao-ti (female)

CHIAO Lin-yi (Party cadre)

Formerly Second Secretary of Secretariat of CCP Canton Municipal Committee.

CHIEN Hsueh-sen (scientist)

Deputy Chairman of National Defense Scientific Committee; Director of Institute of Mechanics, Chinese Academy of Science; an internationally known missile expert who studied in the United States.

CHILINGWANGTAN

From Yunnan Province.

CHIN Tsu-min

CHU Kuang-ya (scientist)
"Responsible person" of National Defense Scientific Committee; a scientist who is believed to have made a significant contribution to development of nuclear weapons in Communist China.

FAN Hsiao-chu (female) (peasant)
Deputy Chairman of Hsiushui County Revolutionary Committee in Kiangsi Province.

FAN Teh-ling

FANG Ming (military, Lin Piao clique)
Chairman of Wuhan Municipal Revolutionary Committee; Commander of Wuhan Garrison.

FANG Yi (+; administrative cadre)
Director of Commission for Economic Relations with Foreign Countries.

FENG Chan-wu

FU Chuan-tso (military)
Air Force Commander of Wuhan Military Region.

HAN Ying

HSIEH Chia-tang

HSIEH Wang-chan (female)

HSU Chih (administrative cadre)
Vice Minister of Metallurgy.

HU Liang-tsai (worker)
Deputy Chairman of Sinkiang Autonomous Region Revolutionary Committee.

HU Wei	(military)	Deputy Chairman of Shensi Provincial Revolutionary Committee; Deputy Commander of Shensi Military District.
HUA Lin-sen		
HUANG Cheng-lien		
HUANG Chih-yung	(military)	Deputy Director of PLA Political Department; Political Commissar of PLA Engineer Corps.
HUANG Jung-hai	(military)	Concurrently Chairman of Canton Municipal Revolutionary Committee and Deputy Chairman of Kwangtung Provincial Revolutionary Committee; Commander of Kwangtung Military District.
HUANG Tso-chen	(military)	Concurrently Deputy Political Commissar of Peking Military Region and Second Political Commissar of Peking Garrison.
HUANG Wen-ming	(military)	Political Commissar of PLA Signal Corps.
JOUTZUTUERHTI		
JUAN Po-sheng	(administrative cadre)	Deputy Chairman of Kirin Provincial Revolutionary Committee; formerly Secretary of Kirin Provincial Party Committee.
KANG Chien-min	(military)	Chairman of Ninghsia Autonomous Region Revolutionary Committee; Political Commissar of Lanchow Military Region.
KANG Lin	(military)	Commander of PLA 28th Army.

KENG Chi-chang (military) Deputy Chairman of Honan Provincial Revolutionary Committee; Second Political Commissar of Hsinhsiang military sub-district.

KUO Hung-chieh

KUO Yu-feng (Party cadre) "Responsible person" of CCP central organization in Peking.

LAN Jung-yu (administrative cadre) Former Deputy Governor of Fukien Province.

LAN Yi-nung (military) Chairman of Kweichow Provincial Revolutionary Committee; "Responsible person" of Kunming Military Region.

LI Hua-min (military) Commander of Wuhan Military Region.

LI Li (administrative cadre) Former Governor of Kweichow Province.

LI Shou-lin (peasant) Member of Standing Committee of Kansu Provincial Revolutionary Committee.

LI Shu-mao (military) Commander of Lanchow Military Region.

LI Ting-shan (administrative cadre) Member of Hupeh Provincial Revolutionary Committee; Chairman of Kuangchi County Revolutionary Committee.

LI Tsai-han (purged) (military, Lin Piao clique) Former Chairman of Kweichow Provincial Revolutionary Committee; Deputy Political Commissar of Kunming Military Region.

LI Yuan (in disgrace) (military, Lin Piao clique) Formerly Chairman of Hunan Provincial Revolutionary Committee; and Commander of Hunan Military District.

LI Yao-sung	(worker)	
LIANG Chin-tang		Deputy Chairman of Kwangtung Provincial Revolutionary Committee.
LIU Chen-hua	(military)	Director of political department of certain PLA army division.
LIU Chun-chiao	(peasant)	From a Hunan commune.
LIU Hao-tien	(military)	First Political Commissar of PLA East Sea Fleet.
LIU Hsi-yao	(administrative cadre)	Vice Chairman of National Defense Scientific Committee.
LO Chun-ti (female)	(peasant)	From Hunan Province.
LO Hsi-kang	(worker)	Member of Standing Committee of Kweichow Provincial Revolutionary Committee.
LO Yuan-fa	(military, Lin Piao clique)	Deputy Commander of PLA Air Force; Air Force Commander at Peking Military Region.
LU Ho	(peasant)	Possibly a member of Heilungkiang Provincial Revolutionary Committee.
LU Ta-tung	(Party cadre)	Deputy Chairman of Chungking Municipal Revolutionary Committee; formerly Second Secretary of Chunking Municipal Party Committee.
LU Tsun-chieh (female)	(Red Guard, Chiang Ching clique)	
LUNG Kuang-chien		Member of Standing Committee of Chinghai Provincial Revolutionary Committee.

MA Tien-shui (Party cadre)
Formerly Secretary of CCP Shanghai Municipal Committee.

NIEH Yuan-tzu (female) (Red Guard, Chiang Ching clique)
Deputy Chairman of Peking Municipal Revolutionary Committee; formerly philosophy instructor at Peking University.

PAN Mei-ying (female) (peasant)
From Kwangsi Province.

PEI Chou-yu (military, Lin Piao clique)
Deputy Political Commissar of Sinkiang Military Region.

PENG Chung (administrative cadre)
Deputy Chairman of Kiangsu Provincial Revolutionary Committee; formerly First Secretary of Nanking Municipal Party Committee.

PENG Kuei-ho (administrative cadre)
Deputy Director of *New China News Agency*.

SHIH Shao-hua (military)
Member of Peking Municipal Revolutionary Committee; combat hero of PLA navy air force unit.

SHU Chi-cheng (military)
Deputy Political Director of a PLA division.

SUNG Shuang-lai (Red Guard)
Deputy Chairman of Chinghai Provincial Revolutionary Committee.

TA Lo (+; military)
Political Commissar of Tsinan Military Region; formerly Secretary of CCP North China Bureau.

TAN Chi-lung (+; military)
Formerly Second Political Commissar of Nanking Military Region.

TANG Liang

TENG Hua	(++; administrative cadre)	Formerly Deputy Governor of Szechuan Province.
TSEN Kuo-jung	(worker)	From Kwangsi Province.
TSENG Yung-ya (in disgrace)	(military)	Former Chairman of Tibet Autonomous Region Revolutionary Committee; Commander of Tibet Military Region.
TSUI Hai-lung	(military)	Deputy Political Commissar of Yenpien Military sub-District in Kirin Province.
TSUI Hsiu-fan	(coal miner)	Deputy Chairman of Liaoning Provincial Revolutionary Committee.
WANG Chia-tao	(military)	Chairman of Heilungkiang Provincial Revolutionary Committee; Commander of Heilungkiang Military District.
WANG Chih-chiang		Deputy Chairman of Ninghsia Autonomous Region Revolutionary Committee.
WANG En-mao	(++; military)	Deputy Chairman of Sinkiang Autonomous Region Revolutionary Committee; former First Party Secretary of Sinkiang and Commander of Sinkiang Military Region.
WANG Hsin	(military)	Deputy Chairman of Honan Provincial Revolutionary Committee; Second Political Commissar of Honan Military District.
WANG Kuang-lin		

WANG Liu-sheng	(military)	Political Commissar of Nanking Military Region.
WANG Ti	(worker, Chiang Ching clique)	Deputy Chairman of Kiangsu Provincial Revolutionary Committee.
WANG Wei-kuo	(military)	Political Commissar of Shanghai Air Force Command.
WEI Tsu-chen		
WEN Hsiang-lan (female)	(peasant)	Member of Standing Committee of Honan Provincial Revolutionary Committee.
WU Chin-chuai	(military, Chiang Ching clique)	Activist in Mao-thought study.
WU Chun-jen	(military)	Deputy Commander of Canton Military Region.
WU Chung	(military)	Deputy Commander of Peking Military Region.
YANG Chun-sheng	(military)	'Responsible person" of Kirin Military District; Commander of PLA 16th Army.
YANG Huan-min	(military)	Air Force Commander of Lanchow Military Region.
YANG Tsung (female)	(peasant)	Deputy head of a commune in Tibet.
YAO Lien-wei	(peasant)	
YEN Chung-chuan	(military)	Deputy Chairman of Kwangtung Provincial Revolutionary Committee; Chief of Staff of Canton Military Region.

YI Yao-tsai	(military)	Marine Commander, North Sea Fleet.
YU Tai-chung	(military)	Chairman of Inner Mongolia Autonomous Regional Revolutionary Committee; formerly Commander of PLA 12th Army.

APPENDIX II

Leaders and Influential Members of the Twenty-Ninth Provincial, Municipal, and Autonomous Regional Revolutionary Committees in Communist China†

(as of August 1971)

Abbreviations:

CC — Central Committee
CCP — Chinese Communist Party
PLA — People's Liberation Army

Name	Position	Description
1. *Heilungkiang Provincial Revolutionary Committee* (established January 31, 1967)		
PAN Fu-sheng (in disgrace)	Original Chairman	Former Political Commissar of Shenyang Military Region and First Political Commissar of Heilungkiang Military District; formerly First Secretary of CCP Heilungkiang Provincial Committee.
WANG Chia-tao	Original Vice-Chairman; Present Chairman	Commander of Heilungkiang Military District.
CHANG Wan-chur	Member	Deputy Commander of Heilungkiang Military District.
KUO Chiang	Member	3rd Political Commissar of Heilungkiang Military District.
FAN Cheng-mei	Member	

† Compiled on the basis of information obtained from various official Chinese Communist media sources, Chinese Nationalist materials, a Hong Kong publication entitled *Current Scene*, and many Western publications.

Name	Position	Description
2. Kirin Provincial Revolutionary Committee (established March 6, 1968)		
WANG Huai-hsiang	Chairman	Deputy Political Commissar of Kirin Military District.
YUAN Po-sheng	Vice-Chairman	Formerly Secretary of Secretariat of CCP Kirin Provincial Committee.
CHENG Chi-chiao	Vice-Chairman	Formerly Alternate Secretary of Secretariat of CCP Kirin Provincial Committee.
HSIAO Tao-sheng	Vice-Chairman	A representative of pro-Mao mass organizations.
HO Yu-fa	Vice-Chairman	Commander of Kirin Military District.
3. Liaoning Provincial Revolutionary Committee (established May 10, 1968)		
CHEN Hsi-lien	Chairman	Commander of Shenyang Military Region.
YANG Chun-fu	Vice-Chairman	Formerly First Secretary of CCP Shenyang Municipal Committee and Secretary of CCP Liaoning Provincial Committee.
LI Po-chu	Vice-Chairman	Deputy Director of Political Department of Shenyang Military Region.

Name	Position	Description
WANG Liang	Vice-Chairman	Formerly Secretary of Secretariat of CCP Liaoning Provincial Committee.
YANG Li	Vice-Chairman	A "responsible person" of a leadership organ of Shenyang Military Region.
YANG Chi	Vice-Chairman	3rd Political Commissar of Shenyang Garrison.
WEI Feng-ying	Vice-Chairman	A "model worker" representative of pro-Mao mass organizations; deputy for Liaoning to 3rd (1964) National People's Congress.
MAO Yuan-hsin	Vice-Chairman	A representative of Red Guards from Harbin Military Engineering College; nephew of Mao Tse-tung.
JEN Pao-cheng	Vice-Chairman	A representative of pro-Mao mass organizations.
TSENG Shao-shan	Vice-Chairman	Political Commissar of Shenyang Military Region.
WANG Feng-en	Vice-Chairman	Member of National People's Congress.
LIU Chung-li	Vice-Chairman	A representative of pro-Mao mass organizations.
YU Kuei-lan	Vice-Chairman	
CHANG Chih-kuo	Vice-Chairman	
WEI Li-ling	Vice-Chairman	
HAO Yi-tien	Vice-Chairman	
LIU Sheng-tien	Vice-Chairman	Member of National People's Congress.

4. *Inner Mongolian Autonomous Regional Revolutionary Committee** (established November 1, 1967)

Name	Position	Description
TENG Hai-ching**	Original Chairman (now removed)	Vice Commander of Peking Military Region and Acting Commander of Inner Mongolian Military District.
YU Tai-chung	Present Chairman	An alternate member of 9th CCP CC; formerly Commander of PLA 12th Army.
WU Tao	Vice-Chairman	Political Commissar of Inner Mongolia Military Region.
KAO Chin-ming	Vice-Chairman	Formerly Secretary of Secretariat of CCP Inner Mongolia Regional Committee.
HUO Tao-yu	Vice-Chairman	Chairman of Revolutionary Committee of No. 1 Building Corporation under 8th Engineering Bureau of Ministry of Building.
LI Shu-te	Member	Formerly Secretary of Secretariat of CCP Inner Mongolia Regional Committee.

* There is an unconfirmed report that the Inner Mongolian Autonomous Region has recently been dismembered and incorporated by the Mao-Lin regime into neighboring provinces, with the Inner Mongolia military region being absorbed by the Lanchow, Peking and Shenyang military regions. According to this report, the above move is made by the Peking regime partly to improve the country's military capacity to oppose the Soviet Union and Outer Mongolia and partly to diminish the troublesome political problem posed China's Mongolian minority. See *The New York Times*, June 21, 1970, p. 7; July 5, 1970, p. 2; and July 22, 1970, p. 5.

** Teng Hai-ching has not been seen in public since May 1970.

5. *Hopeh Provincial Revolutionary Committee* (established February 3, 1968)

LI Hsueh-feng (in disgrace)	Original Chairman	Formerly First Secretary of CCP North China Bureau and of CCP Peking Municipal Committee.
LIU Tzu-hou	Original First Vice-Chairman; Acting Chairman	Formerly First Secretary of CCP Hopeh Provincial Committee and Governor of Hopeh.
MA Hui	Vice-Chairman	Commander of Hopeh Military District.
TSENG Mei	Vice-Chairman	2nd Political Commissar of Hopeh Military District; formerly Commander of Peking Garrison.
CHANG Ying-hui	Vice-Chairman	Commander of PLA 63rd Army stationed in Shihchiachuang.
LIU Tien-chen	Vice-Chairman	A representative of pro-Mao mass organizations; Vice Chairman of Peking Federation of Industry and Commerce.
KENG Chang-so	Vice-Chairman	A "national hero" in agriculture; a representative of pro-Mao mass organizations.

6. *Peking Municipal Revolutionary Committee* (established April 20, 1967)

HSIEH Fu-chih	Chairman	Vice Premier and Minister of Public Security.
WU Te	Vice-Chairman	Formerly Second Secretary of CCP Peking Municipal Committee and Acting Mayor of Peking.

Name	Position	Description
CHENG Wei-shan	Vice-Chairman	Commander of Peking Military Region.
FU Chung-pi	Vice-Chairman	Vice Commander of Peking Military Region and Commander of Peking Garrison. (*Purged in March, 1968.*)
NIEH Yuan-tzu	Vice-Chairman	A representative of pro-Mao Red Guard organization; formerly instructor in philosophy at Peking University.
MOU Li-shan	Member	Standing Committee; a "responsible person" of Peking Area PLA Unit.
NIU Lien-pi	Member	Standing Committee; a representative of pro-Mao mass organizations.
CHOU Jung-kuo	Member	Standing Committee.

7. *Tientsin Municipal Revolutionary Committee* (established December 6, 1967)

Name	Position	Description
HSIEH Hsueh-kung	Chairman	Former Secretary of Secretariat of CCP North China Bureau and First Secretary of CCP Tientsin Municipal Committee.
HSIAO Zsu-ming	Vice-Chairman	2nd Political Commissar of Hopeh Military District and Political Commissar of Tientsin Garrison.

| CHENG San-sheng | Vice-Chairman | Commander of Tientsin Garrison. |
| CHIANG Feng | Vice-Chairman | Director of Tientsin Public Security Bureau. |

8. *Shansi Provincial Revolutionary Committee** (established March 18, 1967)

LIU Ke-ping*	Original Chairman (now removed)	Concurrently Political Commissar of Peking Military Region and First Political Commissar of Shansi Military District; former Vice Governor of Shansi.
HSIEH Cheng-hua*	Present Chairman	Commander of Shansi Military District.
CHANG Jih-ching	Original Vice-Chairman (now removed)	2nd Political Commissar of Peking Military Region and 2nd Political Commissar of Shansi Military District.
LIU Kuan-yi	Vice-Chairman	Formerly Vice Governor of Shansi.
YUAN Chen	Vice-Chairman	Formerly Secretary of Secretariat of CCP Shansi Provincial Committee and First Secretary of CCP Taiyuan Municipal Committee.
CHEN Yung-kuei	Vice-Chairman	A "national labor model"; former Secretary of Party Branch of Tachai Production Brigade, Hsiyang Hsien, Shansi.

* In the spring of 1970, there was a change in the top leadership of the Shansi Provincial Revolutionary Committee, with a loss of position for Maoist extremists. Liu Ke-ping was removed as Chairman, and Chang Ji-ching as Vice-Chairman. The two men have long been at odds. Hsieh Cheng-hua appears to have succeeded Liu as Chairman.

9. *Shantung Provincial Revolutionary Committee** (established February 3, 1967)

Name	Position	Description
WANG Hsiao-yu*	Original Chairman (now removed)	First Political Commissar of Tsinan Military Region and of Shantung Military District; formerly Vice Mayor of Tsingtao.
YANG Te-chih*	Original First Vice-Chairman (now Chairman)	Commander of Tsinan Military Region.
HAN Chih-hai*	Original Vice-Chairman (now removed)	A "responsible person" of Shantung Provincial Revolutionary Workers' Rebel Headquarters.
WANG Chu-chuan*	Original Vice-Chairman (now removed)	A representative of pro-Mao mass organizations.
CHAO Hsiu-teh	Original Vice-Chairman (recently transferred)	Deputy Director of Political Department of Shantung Military District. (He succeeded Fu Chien-wu as Chairman of Tsinan Municipal Revolutionary Committee in 1969, and handed this post over to Hsu Hung-yung recently.)
HSU Hung-yung	Vice-Chairman (recently appointed)	Former Chairman of Tsinan Municipal Revolutionary Committee; formerly Political Commis-

* As a result of major leadership shake-up in the Shantung Provincial Revolutionary Committee in the spring of 1970, with a loss of position for Maoist leftists, Wang Hsiao-yu was removed as Chairman. He is succeeded by Yang Teh-chih. Wang's downfall was followed by a thorough reorganization in Shantung Province from top to bottom to root out the Maoist "rebels."

Name	Position	Description
MU Lin	Vice-Chairman (recently appointed)	sar of PLA Unit 6011 in Kiangsi and a member of the Standing Committee of Kiangsi Provincial Revolutionary Committee.
SU Yi-jan	Vice-Chairman (recently appointed)	Formerly a member of the Secretariat of CCP Shantung Provincial Committee.
YUAN Sheng-ping	Original Member; Vice-Chairman	Former Vice Governor of Shantung; formerly a member of the Secretariat of the CCP Shantung Provincial Committee.
FAN Chao-li	Member (recently appointed)	"Responsible person" of PLA Tsinan Military Region (possibly its Political Commissar).
FU Chia-hsuan	Member (recently appointed)	Deputy Commander of Tsinan Military Region.
LI Yao-wen	Member (recently appointed)	Deputy Commander of Tsinan Military Region.
CHEN Mei-tsao	Member (recently appointed)	"Responsible person" of Tsinan Military Region. (He may have been transferred to the Ministry of Foreign Affairs in Peking.)
PAO Hsien-chih	Member (recently appointed)	Deputy Political Commissar of Tsinan Military Region.
CHENG Shao-fu	Member (recently appointed)	"Responsible person" of Tsinan Military Region; formerly Deputy Political Commissar of Nanking Military Region.
		"Responsible person" of Tsinan Military Region; formerly Deputy Chief of Staff of Peking Military Region.

Name	Position	Description
LIU Yung	Member (recently appointed)	"Responsible person" of Tsinan Military Region.
CHANG Chih-hsiu	Member (recently appointed)	ditto.
TUNG Kuo-kui	Member (recently appointed)	Commander of Shantung Military District.
HO Chih-yuan	Member (recently appointed)	Political Commissar of Shantung Military District.
MA Chung-chuan	Member (recently appointed)	"Responsible person" of PLA units in Shantung.
YANG Kuo-fu	Original member	Deputy Commander of Tsinan Military Region.
YANG Pao-hua	Original member (now removed)	A representative of pro-Mao mass organizations.

10. *Kiangsu Provincial Revolutionary Committee* (established March 23, 1968)

HSU Shih-yu	Chairman	Vice-Minister of National Defense and Commander of Nanking Military Region.
YANG Kuang-li	Vice-Chairman	Concurrently Chairman of Nanking Municipal Revolutionary Committee; a "responsible person" of PLA Unit 6453 in Nanking.
PENG Chung	Vice-Chairman	Formerly Alternate Secretary of Secretariat of CCP Kiangsu Provincial Committee and First Secretary of CCP Nanking Municipal Committee.

WU Ta-sheng	Vice-Chairman	A "responsible person" of Nanking Military Region.
TU Ping	Member	Political Commissar of Nanking Military Region.
PENG Po	Member	

11. *Shanghai Municipal Revolutionary Committee* (established April 20, 1967)

CHANG Chun-chiao	Chairman	Deputy leader of Cultural Revolution Group under CC CCP; First Political Commissar of Nanking Military Region and of Shanghai Garrison; formerly Secretary of Secretariat of CCP Shanghai Municipal Committee.
YAO Wen-yuan	Vice-Chairman	Member of Cultural Revolution Group under CC CCP; formerly Editor-in-Chief of Shanghai *Liberation Daily.*
LIAO Cheng-kuo	Vice-Chairman	Commander of Shanghai Garrison.
MA Tien-shui	Vice-Chairman	Former Secretary of Secretariat of CCP Shanghai Municipal Committee.
WANG Hung-wen	Vice-Chairman	A workers' representative.
WANG Hsiu-chun	Vice-Chairman	A woman worker.
CHOU Chun-lin	Vice-Chairman	Commander of Shanghai Garrison.
WANG Shao-yung	Vice-Chairman	Formerly Alternate Secretary of Secretariat of CCP Shanghai Municipal Committee.
HSU Ching-hsien	Vice-Chairman	

Name	Position	Description
12. *Anhwei Provincial Revolutionary Committee* (established April 18, 1968)		
LI Te-sheng*	Chairman	Commander of Anhwei Military District and PLA Unit 6408 (12th Army).
LIAO Cheng-mei	Vice-Chairman	A "responsible person" of PLA Unit 6408.
SUNG Pei-chang	Vice-Chairman	Deputy Political Commissar of Anhwei Military District; a "responsible person" of PLA Unit 6408.
LI Jen-chih	Vice-Chairman	Formerly Secretary of Secretariat of CCP Anhwei Provincial Committee and Vice Governor of Anhwei.
YANG Hsiao-chun	Vice-Chairman	Formerly member of Standing Committee of CCP Anhwei Provincial Committee.
HSU Wen-cheng	Vice-Chairman	A representative of pro-Mao mass organizations.
CHANG Hsiu-ying	Vice-Chairman	
CHANG Chia-yun	Vice-Chairman	
13. *Chekiang Provincial Revolutionary Committee* (established March 24, 1968)		
NAN Ping	Chairman	Acting Political Commissar of Chekiang Military District.

*Li Te-sheng recently became Director of the General Political Department of the Chinese People's Liberation Army. He also holds the concurrent posts of Chairman of the Anhwei Provincial Revolutionary Committee and Commander of the Anhwei Military District.

CHEN Li-yun — First Vice-Chairman — Political Commissar of PLA Air Force Unit 7350 in Chekiang area.

LAI Ko-ko — Vice-Chairman — Former Secretary of Secretariat of CCP Chekiang Provincial Committee.

HSIUNG Ying-tang — Vice-Chairman — Commander of Chekiang Military District and PLA Unit 6409.

CHOU Chien-jen — Vice-Chairman — Formerly non-Communist Governor of Chekiang.

WANG Tzu-ta — Vice-Chairman — Concurrently Chairman of Hangchow Municipal Revolutionary Committee; formerly Alternate Secretary of Secretariat of CCP Municipal Committee and Mayor of Hangchow.

HUA Yin-feng — Vice-Chairman — A "model peasant"; a representative of pro-Mao mass organizations.

14. *Fukien Provincial Revolutionary Committee* (established August 19, 1968)

HAN Hsien-chu — Chairman — Commander of Foochow Military Region; Deputy Chief of General Staff, PLA.

PI Ting-chun — Vice-Chairman — Deputy Commander of Foochow Military Region.

LAN Jung-yu — Vice-Chairman — Formerly Vice Governor of Fukien.

CHU Yao-hua — Vice-Chairman — Commander of Fukien Military District.

Name	Position	Description
15. *Kiangsi Provincial Revolutionary Committee* (established January 5, 1968)		
CHENG Shih-ching	Chairman	Vice Political Commissar of Foochow Military Region and Political Commissar of Kiangsi Military District; formerly Commander and Political Commissar of Yentai (Chefoo) Military Subdistrict, Shantung.
YANG Tung-liang	Vice-Chairman	Commander of Kiangsi Military District.
HUANG Hsien	Vice-Chairman	Formerly Alternate Secretary of Secretariat of CCP Provincial Committee and Vice Governor of Kiangsi.
PAI Tung-tsai	Vice-Chairman	A veteran party leader and agricultural specialist.
YU Hou-te	Vice-Chairman	A representative of pro-Mao mass organizations.
WANG Li-liang	Vice-Chairman	
16. *Honan Provincial Revolutionary Committee* (established January 31, 1967)		
LIU Chien-hsun	Chairman	Concurrently Political Commissar of Wuhan Military Region and First Political Commissar of Honan Military District; formerly First Secretary of CCP Honan Provincial Committee.

Name	Position	Description
WANG Hsin	Vice-Chairman	2nd Political Commissar of Honan Military District.
CHI Teng-kuei	Vice-Chairman	Formerly Alternate Secretary of Secretariat of CCP Honan Provincial Committee.
KENG Chi-chang	Vice-Chairman	
YANG Li-yung	Vice-Chairman	Political Commissar of PLA Unit 8172 in Kaifeng.
CHANG Shu-chih	Member	Commander of Honan Military District.

17. *Hupeh Provincial Revolutionary Committee* (established February 5, 1968)

Name	Position	Description
TSENG Szu-yu	Chairman	Commander of Wuhan Military Region; formerly Lin Piao's chief personal bodyguard during the Long March.
LIU Feng	Vice-Chairman	Political Commissar of Wuhan Military Region.
CHANG Ti-hsueh	Vice-Chairman	Political Commissar of Hupeh Military District; formerly Second Secretary of CCP Provincial Committee and Governor of Hupeh.
JEN Ai-sheng	Vice-Chairman	Former Director of Rural Work Department of CCP Hupeh Provincial Committee.
LIANG Jen-kuei	Vice-Chairman	Deputy Commander of Hupeh Military District.
CHU Hung-hsia	Vice-Chairman	A representative of pro-Mao mass organizations.

Name	Position	Description
JAO Hsing-li	Vice-Chairman	Vice Chairman of Hupeh Provincial Association of Poor and Lower-Middle Peasants.
YANG Tao-yuan	Vice-Chairman	A representative of pro-Mao mass organizations.
CHANG Li-kuo	Vice-Chairman	

18. *Hunan Provincial Revolutionary Committee* (established April 8, 1968)

Name	Position	Description
LI Yuan*	Original Chairman (now removed)	Commander of PLA Unit 6900 (47th Army) stationed in Hunan.
LUNG Shu-chin**	First Vice-Chairman	Commander of Hunan Military District.
HUA Kuo-feng*	Originally Vice-Chairman, but now Acting Chairman	Formerly Secretary of Secretariat of CCP Provincial Committee and Vice Governor of Hunan.
YANG Ta-yi	Vice-Chairman	A "responsible person" of Hunan Military District.
PU Chan-ya	Vice-Chairman	First Political Commissar of Hunan Military District.

* Li Yuan has not been seen in public for some months. Indications are that he has been in disgrace. Hua Kuo-feng apparently succeeded him as Acting Chairman. When the new Hunan Provincial Party Committee was established in December 1970, Hua Kuo-feng was appointed its First Secretary, Pu Chan-ya and Yang Ta-yi were made secretary and deputy secretary. Li Yuan was not mentioned.

** In the summer of 1968, Lung was transferred to Sinkiang province to become Chairman of the Sinkiang Uighur Autonomous Regional Revolutionary Committee. His successor has not yet been officially named.

CHANG Po-sen	Vice-Chairman	Formerly Alternate Secretary of Secretariat of CCP Provincial Committee and Vice Governor of Hunan.
LIU Shun-wen	Vice-Chairman	A representative of pro-Mao mass organizations.
HU Yung	Vice-Chairman	A representative of pro-Mao mass organizations.
YEH Wei-tung	Vice-Chairman	
CHENG Po	Member	A "responsible person" of PLA Unit 6900 in Changsha area.

19. *Kwantung Provincial Revolutionary Committee* (established February 21, 1968)

HUANG Yung-sheng*	Original Chairman (transferred to Peking)	PLA Chief of General Staff; former Commander of Canton Military Region.
LIU Hsing-yuan*	Present Chairman	Deputy Political Commissar of Canton Military Region.
KUNG Shih-chuan	First Vice-Chairman	3rd Political Commissar of Canton Military Region.
CHEN Yu	Vice-Chairman	Formerly Secretary of Secretariat of CCP Provincial Committee and Governor of Kwangtung.

* Huang Yung-sheng became PLA Chief of General Staff in March 1968, and Liu Hsing-yuan succeeded him in 1969.

Name	Position	Description
WANG Shou-tao	Vice-Chairman	Former Secretary of Secretariat of CCP Central-South China Bureau.
CHIU Kuo-kuang	Vice-Chairman	Vice-Commander of Canton Military Region.
YEN Chung-chuan	Vice-Chairman	Chief of Staff of Canton Military Region.
HUANG Jung-hai	Vice-Chairman	Concurrently Chairman of Canton Municipal Revolutionary Committee; Commander of Kwangtung Military District.
LIU Chi-fa	Vice-Chairman	A worker of Canton Heavy Duty Machine Works and a member of its Red Flag group.
HUANG Yu-ying	Vice-Chairman	A primary school teacher in a commune of Chiehyang Hsien, Kwangtung.
CHEN Te	Member	Political Commissar of Kwangtung Military District; Deputy Commander of Canton Military District.
LIN Li-ming	Member	Formerly Second Secretary of CCP Provincial Committee and Acting Governor of Kwangtung.
PAI Ping	Member	Deputy Political Commissar of Kwangtung Military District.

20. *Kwangsi Autonomous Regional Revolutionary Committee* (established August 26, 1968)

WEI Kuo-ching	Chairman	First Political Commissar of Kwangsi Military District; formerly Secretary of Secretariat of CCP Central-South China Bureau.
OU Chih-fu	Vice-Chairman	Commander of Kwangsi Military District.
AN Ping-sheng	Vice-Chairman	A former Party official.
WEI Yu-chu	Vice-Chairman	3rd Political Commissar of Kwangsi Military District.
LIU Chung-kuei	Vice-Chairman	Deputy Commander of Kwangsi Military District.

21. *Shensi Provincial Revolutionary Committee* (established May 1, 1968)

LI Jui-shan	Chairman	Formerly Secretary of Secretariat of CCP Hunan Provincial Committee and First Secretary of CCP Changsha Municipal Committee.
HU Wei	Vice-Chairman	Political Commissar of Shensi Military District; a "responsible person" of PLA Unit 8133 in Sian Area.
HUANG Ching-yao	Vice-Chairman	Commander of Shensi Military District; formerly Vice-Commander of Heilungkiang Military District.
HSIAO Chun	Vice-Chairman	Former Secretary of Secretariat of CCP Shensi Provincial Committee and First Secretary of CCP Sian Municipal Committee.

Name	Position	Description
CHANG Pei-hsin	Vice-Chairman	A representative of pro-Mao mass organizations.
MA Hsi-sheng	Vice-Chairman	A representative of pro-Mao mass organizations.
SHAN Ying-chieh	Vice-Chairman	A representative of pro-Mao mass organizations.
WANG Feng-chin	Vice-Chairman	Member of National People's Congress.
LI Shih-ying	Vice-Chairman	A representative of pro-Mao mass organizations.
SUN Fu-lin	Vice-Chairman	A representative of pro-Mao mass organizations.
YANG Meng-yuan	Vice-Chairman	A representative of pro-Mao mass organizations.

22. *Ninghsia Autonomous Regional Revolutionary Committee* (established April 10, 1968)

Name	Position	Description
KANG Chien-min	Chairman	Deputy Political Commissar of Lanchow Military Region.
CHANG Huai-li	Vice-Chairman	Deputy Commander of Ninghsia Military District.
HSU Hung-hsueh	Vice-Chairman	A "responsible person" of Ninghsia PLA Support-Left Committee.

| WANG Chih-chiang | Vice-Chairman | Vice-Chairman of People's Council of Ninghsia Hui Autonomous Region. |
| AN Chien-kuo | Vice-Chairman | A representative of pro-Mao mass organizations. |

23. *Kansu Provincial Revolutionary Committee* (established January 24, 1968)

HSIEN Heng-han	Chairman	Political Commissar of Lanchow Military Region.
CHANG Chung	Vice-Chairman	Deputy Commander of Kansu Military District.
HU Chi-tsung	Vice-Chairman	Formerly Secretary of Secretariat of CCP Provincial Committee and Vice-Governor of Kansu.
PI Ting-chun	Vice-Chairman	Deputy Commander of Foochow Military Region.
CHIU Yu-min	Vice-Chairman	A representative of "revolutionary" workers.
HSIAO Tse-min	Vice-Chairman	A representative of pro-Mao mass organizations.
HSU Kuo-chen	Vice-Chairman	Deputy Commander of Lanchow Military Region.

24. *Tsinghai Provincial Revolutionary Committee* (established August 12, 1967)

| LIU Hsien-chuan | Chairman | Deputy Commander of Lanchow Military Region; Commander of Tsinghai Military District. |

Name	*Position*	*Description*
CHANG Chiang-lin	First Vice-Chairman	Deputy Commander of Tsinghai Military District.
HSUEH Hung-fu	Vice-Chairman	Formerly Alternate Secretary of Secretariat of CCP Tsinghai Provincial Committee.
MAO Chi-wen	Vice-Chairman	Member of Standing Committee of Tsinghai Provincial "August 18" Revolutionary Rebels Alliance Committee.
LIU Ming-chien	Vice-Chairman	Member of Standing Committee of Tsinghai Provincial "August 18" Revolutionary Rebels Alliance Committee.
WANG Chung-shan	Vice-Chairman	Member of Standing Committee of Tsinghai Provincial "August 18" Revolutionary Rebels Alliance Committee.
TA Lo	Vice-Chairman	A Tibetan; Vice-Dean of Stockbreeding and Veterinary College of Tsinghai University; Chairman of Revolutionary Committee of Tsinghai University.

25. Sinkiang Uighur Autonomous Regional Revolutionary Committee (established September 5, 1968)

LUNG Shu-chin	Chairman	Commander of Sinkiang Military Region.
WANG En-mao	Vice-Chairman	Formerly First Secretary of CCP Sinkiang Autonomous Regional Committee and Commander of Sinkiang Military Region.

SAIFUDIN	Vice-Chairman	Deputy Commander of Sinkiang Military Region.
KUO Peng	Vice-Chairman	Deputy Commander of Sinkiang Military Region.
PEI Chou-yu	Vice-Chairman	Deputy Political Commissar of Sinkiang Production-Construction Corps.
LI Chuan-chun	Vice-Chairman	Commander of PLA Unit 7335.

26. *Szechwan Provincial Revolutionary Committee* (established May 31, 1968)

CHANG Kuo-hua	Chairman	First Political Commissar of Chengtu Military Region.
LIANG Hsing-chu	Vice-Chairman	Commander of Chengtu Military Region.
LIU Chieh-ting	Vice-Chairman	Deputy Political Commissar of Chengtu Military Region; formerly Secretary of CCP Ipin District Committee.
CHANG Hsi-ting (Mrs. Liu Chieh-ting)	Vice-Chairman	Former Secretary of CCP Ipin Municipal Committee.

27. *Kweichow Provincial Revolutionary Committee** (established February 13, 1967)

LI Tsai-han*	Original Chairman (now removed)	Deputy Political Commissar of Kunming Military Region and First Political Commissar of Kweichow Military District.

* As a result of change in the top leadership of the Kweichow Provincial Revolutionary Committee in the spring of 1970, with a loss of position for Maoist radicals, Li Tsai-han was removed as Chairman. Lan Yi-nung succeeded Li.

Name	Position	Description
LAN Yi-nung*	Present Chairman	"Responsible person" of Kunming Military Region.
CHANG Ming	Vice-Chairman	Director of Kweichow Bureau of Material Supply.
LI Li	Vice-Chairman	Former Secretary of CCP Provincial Committee and Governor of Kweichow.
SUN Chang-te	Vice-Chairman	Member of Geochemical Research Institute of Chinese Academy of Sciences.
LIU An-min	Vice-Chairman	Political Commissar of Logistics Department of Kweichow Military District.
HO Kuang-yu	Vice-Chairman	Commander of Kweichow Military District.
TIEN Hua-yi	Member	Deputy Political Commissar of Kweichow Military District.

28. *Yunnan Provincial Revolutionary Committee* (established August 13, 1968)

Name	Position	Description
TAN Fu-jen** (died)	Chairman	Political Commissar of Kunming Military Region; formerly Chief Judge of Supreme Military Court and Political Commissar of PLA Engineer Corps.

* As a result of change in the top leadership of the Kweichow Provincial Revolutionary Committee in the spring of 1970, with a loss of position for Maoist radicals, Li Tsai-han was removed as Chairman. Lan Yi-nung succeeded Li.

** According to the March 9, 1971 issue of the *Hong Kong Times*, Tan Fu-jen was killed by an anti-Communist in Kunming in December, 1970.

Name	Position	Description
CHOU Hsing	Original Vice-Chairman; Present Chairman	Political Commissar of Yunnan Military District; formerly Secretary of CCP Provincial Committee and Governor of Yunnan.
CHEN Kang	Vice-Chairman	Deputy Commander of Kunming Military Region.
LU Jui-lin	Vice-Chairman	Deputy Commander of Kunming Military Region.

29. *Tibetan Autonomous Regional Revolutionary Committee* (established September 5, 1968)

Name	Position	Description
TSENG Yung-ya (in disgrace)	Original Chairman	Commander of Tibet Military Region.
JEN Jung	Original Vice-Chairman; Acting Chairman	Deputy Political Commissar of Tibet Military Region.
CHEN Ming-yi	Vice-Chairman	Deputy Commander of Tibet Military Region.
LIAO Pu-yun	Vice-Chairman	Deputy Commander of Tibet Military Region.
Ngapo Ngawang-Jigme	Vice-Chairman	Tibetan; formerly chief minister under Dalai Lama.
T'ien Pao	Vice-Chairman	Tibetan; "Responsible person" of the Tibetan Military Region; former Vice-Governor of Szechuan Province.

APPENDIX III

Leaders of the Twenty-Nine Provincial Muncipal, Autonomous Regional Party Committees in Communist China (as of August 1971)*

Name	Position	Concurrent Posts Held
1. *Hunan Provincial Party Committee* (established in December 1970)		
HUA Ko-feng	First Secretary	Acting Chairman of Hunan Provincial Revolutionary Committee; formerly Secretary of Secretariat of CCP Provincial Committee and Vice-Governor of Hunan.
PU Chan-ya	Secretary	Vice-Chairman of Hunan Provincial Revolutionary Committee; First Political Commissar of Hunan Military District.
YANG Ta-yi	Deputy Secretary	Vice-Chairman of Hunan Provincial Revolutionary Committee; Commander of Hunan Military District.

* See *New China News Agency*, December 14, 1970; May 24, 1971; May 30, 1971; June 8, 1971; August 24, 1971; August 25, 1971; *Free China Weekly*, Taipei, Taiwan, February 28, 1971, p. 2; *Peking Review*, December 25, 1970, p. 4; January 8, 1971, p. 5; January 22, 1971, p. 3; February 5, 1971, p. 4; February 26, 1971, pp. 4–5; April 2, 1971, pp. 19–20; and April 23, 1971, pp. 19–20; *The New York Times*, December 15, 1970, p. 13; January 2, 1971, p. 3; January 17, 1971, p. 5; February 7, 1971, p. 18; February 23, 1971, p. 13; March 21, 1971, p. 9; March 28, 1971, p. 20; and May 26, 1971, p. 12; and *The Washington Post*, December 16, 1970, p. 20; February 22, 1971, p. 14; and March 21, 1971, p. 31.

2. *Kwangtung Provincial Party Committee* (established in December 1970)

LIU Hsing-yuan	First Secretary	Chairman of Kwangtung Provincial Revolutionary Committee; First Political Commissar of Canton Military Region.
KUNG Shih-chuan	Secretary	First Vice-Chairman of Kwangtung Provincial Revolutionary Committee; 2nd Political Commissar of Canton Military Region.
TING Sheng	Secretary	Vice-Chairman of Kwangtung Provincial Revolutionary Committee; a "responsible person" of Canton Military Region.
CHEN Yu	Secretary	Vice-Chairman of Kwangtung Provincial Revolutionary Committee; formerly Secretary of Secretariat of CCP Provincial Committee and Governor of Kwangtung.
WANG Shou-tao	Secretary	Vice-Chairman of Kwangtung Provincial Revolutionary Committee; formerly Secretary of CCP Central-South China Bureau.

3. *Kiangsu Provincial Party Committee* (established in December 1970)

HSU Shih-yu	First Secretary	Chairman of Kiangsu Provincial Revolutionary Committee; Commander of Nanking Military Region.
TU Ping	Secretary	Political Commissar of Nanking Military Region.

Name	Position	Concurrent Posts Held
WU Ta-sheng	Secretary	Vice-Chairman of Kiangsu Provincial Revolutionary Committee; First Political Commissar of Kiangsu Military District.
PENG Chun	Deputy Secretary	Vice-Chairman of Kiangsu Provincial Revolutionary Committee; formerly Alternate Secretary of Secretariat of Kiangsu Provincial Committee of CCP.
YANG Kuang-li	Deputy Secretary	Vice-Chairman of Kiangsu Provincial Revolutionary Committee; a "responsible person" of PLA Unit 6453 in Nanking; Chairman of Nanking Municipal Revolutionary Committee.

4. *Kiangsi Provincial Party Committee* (established in December 1970)

Name	Position	Concurrent Posts Held
CHEN Shih-ching	First Secretary	Chairman of Kiangsi Provincial Revolutionary Committee; Vice Political Commissar of Foochow Military Region; Political Commissar of Kiangsi Military District.
YANG Tung-liang	Secretary	Vice-Chairman of Kiangsi Provincial Revolutionary Committee; Commander of Kiangsi Military District.
PAI Tung-tsai	Deputy Secretary	Vice-Chairman of Kiangsi Provincial Revolutionary Committee; an old Party leader and agricultural specialist.

WEN Tao-hung	Deputy Secretary	Deputy Political Commissar of Kiangsi Military District.

5. *Shanghai Municipal Party Committee* (established in January 1971)

CHANG Chun-chao	First Secretary	Chairman of Shanghai Municipal Revolutionary Committee; First Political Commissar of Nanking Military Region and Shanghai Garrison.
YAO Wen-yuan	Second Secretary	Deputy Chairman of Shanghai Municipal Revolutionary Committee; a Regular Member of Politburo of 9th CCP CC.
WANG Hung-wen	Secretary	Vice-Chairman of Shanghai Municipal Revolutionary Committee; in charge of Shanghai Department of Industry; a member of No. 17 State Cotton Mill; a Regular Member of 9th CCP CC.
CHOU Shun-lin	Secretary	Vice-Chairman of Shanghai Municipal Revolutionary Committee; Commander of Shanghai Garrison.
HSU Ching-hsien	Secretary	Vice-Chairman of Shanghai Municipal Revolutionary Committee.
WANG Hsiu-chen	Secretary	Vice-Chairman of Shanghai Municipal Revolutionary Committee; a woman worker of No. 30 State Cotton Mill.

Name	Position	*Concurrent* Posts Held
6. *Anhwei Provincial Party Committee* (established in January 1971)		
LI Teh-sheng	First Secretary	Chairman of Anhwei Provincial Revolutionary Committee; Head of PLA's General Political Department; Commander of Anhwei Military District.
SUNG Pei-chang	Secretary	Vice-Chairman of Anhwei Provincial Revolutionary Committee; Deputy Political Commissar of Anhwei Military District.
LI Jen-chih	Deputy Secretary	Vice-Chairman of Anhwei Provincial Revolutionary Committee.
LIANG Chi-ching	Deputy Secretary	Political Commissar of Anhwei Military District.
KUO Hung-chieh	Deputy Secretary	Secretary of Kuo-chuang Brigade Party Branch at Poli Commune in Hsiao Hsien.
7. *Chekiang Provincial Party Committee* (established in January 1971)		
NAN Ping	First Secretary	Chairman of Chekiang Provincial Revolutionary Committee; Acting Political Commissar of Chekiang Military District.
CHEN Li-yun	Secretary	First Vice-Chairman of Chekiang Provincial Revolutionary Committee; Political Commissar of PLA Air Force Unit 7350 in Chekiang area.

HSIUNG Ying-targ	Secretary	Vice-Chairman of Chekiang Provincial Revolutionary Committee; Commander of Chekiang Military District and PLA Unit 6409.
LAI Ko-ko	Deputy Secretary	Vice-Chairman of Chekiang Provincial Revolutionary Committee; formerly Secretary of Secretariat of CCP Chekiang Provincial Committee.
HSIEH Cheng-hao	Deputy Secretary	A "responsible person" of PLA Units in Shanghai.
CHAI Chi-kun	Deputy Secretary	A military officer.

8. *Kwangsi Chuang Autonomous Regional Party Committee* (established in February 1971)

WEI Kuo-ching	First Secretary	Chairman of Kwangsi Autonomous Regional Revolutionary Committee; First Political Commissar of Kwangsi Military District.
WEI Tsu-chen	Secretary	A military officer.
LIU Chung-kuei	Deputy Secretary	Vice-Chairman of Kwangsi Autonomous Regional Revolutionary Committee; Deputy Commander of Kwangsi Military District.
AN Ping-sheng	Deputy Secretary	Vice-Chairman of Kwangsi Autonomous Regional Revolutionary Committee; a veteran Party official.

Name	Position	Concurrent Posts Held
9. *Kansu Provincial Party Committee* (established in February 1971)		
HSIEN Heng-han	First Secretary	Chairman of Kansu Provincial Revolutionary Committee; Political Commissar of Lanchow Military Region.
PI Ting-chun	Secretary	Vice-Chairman of Kansu Provincial Revolutionary Committee; Deputy Commander of Foochow Military Region.
HU Chi-tsung	Secretary	Vice-Chairman of Kansu Provincial Revolutionary Committee; formerly Secretary of Secretariat of CCP Provincial Committee and Vice-Governor of Kansu.
10. *Liaoning Provincial Party Committee* (established in January 1971)		
CHEN Hsi-lien	First Secretary	Chairman of Liaoning Provincial Revolutionary Committee; Commander of Shenyang Military Region.
TSENG Shao-shan	Second Secretary	Vice-Chairman of Liaoning Provincial Revolutionary Committee; Political Commissar of Shenyang Military Region.
LI Po-chiu	Secretary	Vice-Chairman of Liaoning Provincial Revolutionary Committee; Deputy Director of Political Department of Shenyang Military Region.

| YANG Chun-fu | Deputy Secretary | Vice-Chairman of Liaoning Provincial Revolutionary Committee; formerly First Secretary of CCP Shenyang Municipal Committee and Secretary of CCP Liaoning Provincial Committee. |
| MAO Yuan-hsin | Deputy Secretary | Vice-Chairman of Liaoning Provincial Revolutionary Committee; a representative of Red Guards from Harbin Military Engineering College. (Mao Tse-tung's nephew.) |

11. *Peking Municipal Party Committee* (established in March 1971)

HSIEH Fu-chih	First Secretary	Chairman of Peking Municipal Revolutionary Committee; Deputy Premier; Minister of Public Security.
WU Teh	Second Secretary	Vice-Chairman of Peking Municipal Revolutionary Committee.
YANG Chun-sheng	Secretary	"Responsible person" of Kirin Military District; Commander of PLA 16th Army.
WU Chung	Secretary	Deputy Commander of Peking Military Region.
HUANG Tso-chen	Secretary	Deputy Political Commissar of Peking Military Region; 2nd Political Commissar of Peking Garrison.
LIU Shao-wen	Secretary	3rd Political Commissar of Peking Garrison.
TING Kuo-yu	Secretary	Former ambassador to Pakistan.

Name	Position	Concurrent Posts Held
12. *Shensi Provincial Party Committee* (established in March 1971)		
LI Jui-shan	First Secretary	Chairman of Shensi Provincial Revolutionary Committee.
HU Wei	Secretary	Vice-Chairman of Shensi Provincial Revolutionary Committee; Political Commissar of Shensi Military District.
HUANG Ching-yao	Secretary	Vice-Chairman of Shensi Provincial Revolutionary Committee; Commander of Shensi Military District.
HSIAO Chun	Deputy Secretary	Vice-Chairman of Shensi Provincial Revolutionary Committee.
WU Kuei-hsien (female)	Deputy Secretary	A textile worker; Member of Shensi Provincial Revolutionary Committee. (Chiang Ching clique)
13. *Honan Provincial Party Committee* (established in March 1971)		
LIU Chien-hsun	First Secretary	Chairman of Honan Provincial Revolutionary Committee; Political Commissar of Wuhan Military Region; 1st Political Commissar of Honan Military District.
WANG Hsin	Secretary	Vice-Chairman of Honan Provincial Revolutionary Committee; 2nd Political Commissar of Honan Military District.

CHI Teng-kuei	Secretary	Vice-Chairman of Honan Provincial Revolutionary Committee; a Party cadre.
KENG Chi-chang	Secretary	Vice-Chairman of Honan Provincial Revolutionary Committee.
CHANG Shu-chih	Secretary	Commander of Honan Military District; Member of Honan Provincial Revolutionary Committee.

14. *Tsinghai Provincial Party Committee* (established in March 1971)

LIU Hsien-chuan	First Secretary	Chairman of Tsinghai Provincial Revolutionary Committee; Deputy Commander of Lanchow Military Region.
CHANG Chiang-lin	Second Secretary	1st Vice-Chairman of Tsinghai Provincial Revolutionary Committee; Deputy Commander of Tsinghai Military District.
SUNG Chang-keng	Secretary	Political Commissar of Tsinghai Military District.
HSUEH Hung-fu	Deputy Secretary	Vice-Chairman of Tsinghai Provincial Revolutionary Committee.
LU Chinh-an	Deputy Secretary	Vice-Chairman of Tsinghai Provincial Revolutionary Committee; Member of Standing Committee of Tsinghai Provincial "August 18" Revolutionary Rebels Alliance Committee.

Name	Position	Concurrent Posts Held
TA Lo	Deputy Secretary	Vice-Chairman of Tsinghai Provincial Revolutionary Committee; Chairman of Revolutionary Committee of Tsinghai University.

15. *Kirin Provincial Party Committee* (established in March 1971)

Name	Position	Concurrent Posts Held
WANG Huai-hsiang	First Secretary	Chairman of Kirin Provincial Revolutionary Committee; Deputy Commander of Kirin Military District.
CHANG Chao-jen	Secretary	
HO Yu-fa	Secretary	Vice-Chairman of Kirin Provincial Revolutionary Committee; Commander of Kirin Military District.
HSIAO Tao-sheng	Secretary	Vice-Chairman of Kirin Provincial Revolutionary Committee; a representative of pro-Mao mass organizations.
CHENG Chi-chiao	Secretary	Vice-Chairman of Kirin Provincial Revolutionary Committee; a Party cadre.
YUAN Po-sheng	Secretary	Vice-Chairman of Kirin Provincial Revolutionary Committee; a Party cadre.

16. *Hupeh Provincial Party Committee* (established in March 1971)

Name	Position	Concurrent Posts Held
TSENG Szu-yu	First Secretary	Chairman of Hupeh Provincial Revolutionary Committee; Commander of Wuhan Military Region.

LIU Feng	Second Secretary	Vice-Chairman of Hupeh Provincial Revolutionary Committee; Political Commissar of Wuhan Military Region.
CHANG Ti-hsueh	Secretary	Vice-Chairman of Hupeh Provincial Revolutionary Committee; Political Commissar of Hupeh Military District.
CHANG Yu-hua	Secretary	Deputy Political Commissar of Wuhan Military Region.
KUNG Ching-teh	Secretary	Deputy Commander of Wuhan Military Region.
CHIANG Yi	Secretary	Deputy Political Commissar of PLA units in Wuhan.
PAN Chen-wu	Secretary	

17. *Fukien Provincial Party Committee* (established March 1971)

HAN Hsien-chu	First Secretary	Chairman of Fukien Provincial Revolutionary Committee; Commander of Foochow Military Region; Deputy Chief of PLA General Staff.
CHOU Chih-ping	Second Secretary	Political Commissar of Foochow Military Region.
CHO Hsiung	Secretary	
TAN Chi-lung	Secretary	Political Commissar of Tsinan Military Region.
CHU Shao-ching	Secretary	"Responsible person" of Foochow Military Region.

Name	*Position*	*Concurrent Posts Held*
HUANG Ya-kuang	Secretary	
NI Nan-shan	Secretary	

18. *Shantung Provincial Party Committee* (established in March 1971)

Name	*Position*	*Concurrent Posts Held*
YANG Teh-chih	First Secretary	Chairman of Shantung Provincial Revolutionary Committee; Commander of Tsinan Military Region.
YUAN Sheng-ping	Second Secretary	Vice-Chairman of Shantung Provincial Revolutionary Committee; "Responsible person" of Tsinan Military Region.
CHANG Chih-hsiu	Deputy Secretary	Member of Shantung Provincial Revolutionary Committee; "Responsible person" of Tsinan Military Region.
PAI Ju-sing	Deputy Secretary	
SU Yi-jan	Deputy Secretary	Vice-Chairman of Shantung Provincial Revolutionary Committee; an administrative cadre.

19. *Shansi Provincial Party Committee* (established in March 1971)

Name	*Position*	*Concurrent Posts Held*
HSIEH Chen-hua	First Secretary	Chairman of Shansi Provincial Revolutionary Committee; Commander of Shansi Military District.
TSAO Chung-nan	Secretary	Vice-Chairman of Shansi Provincial Revolutionary Committee; "Responsible person" of Shansi Military District.

CHEN Yung-kuei	Secretary	Vice-Chairman of Shansi Provincial Revolutionary Committee; a "national labor model."
CHANG Ping-hua	Secretary	Formerly 1st Secretary of CCP Hunan Provincial Party Committee, and Vice-Minister of Propaganda. (Formerly Tao Chu's clique)

20. *Sinkiang-Uighur Autonomous Party Committee* (established in May 1971)

LUNG Shu-chin	First Secretary	Chairman of Sinkiang Autonomous Regional Revolutionary Committee; Commander of Sinkiang Military Region.
SAIFUDIN	Second Secretary	Vice-Chairman of Sinkiang Autonomous Regional Revolutionary Committee; Deputy Commander of Sinkiang Military Region.
SUNG Chih-ho	Secretary	Formerly Vice-Minister of Allocation of Materials.
LIU Hsing	Secretary	Formerly Vice-Minister of 6th Ministry of Machine Building.
HSIAO Ssu-ming	Secretary	A military officer.

21. *Kweichow Provincial Party Committee* (established in May 1971)

LAN Yi-nung	First Secretary	Chairman of Kweichow Provincial Revolutionary Committee; "Responsible person" of Kunming Military Region.

Name	*Position*	*Concurrent Posts Held*
CHANG Jun-sen	Secretary	A military officer.
CHIA Ting-san	Deputy Secretary	A Party cadre.
LI Li	Deputy Secretary	A Party cadre.
HO Kuang-yu	Deputy Secretary	Vice-Chairman of Kweichow Provincial Revolutionary Committee; Commander of Kweichow Military District.

22. *Inner Mongolian Autonomous Regional Party Committee* (established in May 1971)

YU Tai-chung	First Secretary	Chairman of Inner Mongolian Autonomous Regional Revolutionary Committee; formerly Commander of PLA 12th Army.
WU Tao	Secretary	Vice-Chairman of Inner Mongolian Autonomous Regional Revolutionary Committee.
HSU Hsin	Secretary	
TENG Tsun-len	Secretary	
CHAO Tzu-yang	Secretary	

23. *Hopeh Provincial Party Committee* (established in May 1971)

LI Tzu-hou	First Secretary	Acting Chairman of Hopeh Provincial Revolutionary Committee; a Party cadre.
CHENG San-sheng	Second Secretary	A "responsible person" of PLA units in Tientsin.

MA Hui	Secretary	Vice-Chairman of Hopeh Provincial Revolutionary Committee; Commander of Hopeh Military District.
LIU Hai-ching	Secretary	
MA Chieh	Secretary	
LU Yu-lan (female)	Deputy Secretary	
MA Li	Deputy Secretary	

24. *Tientsin Municipal Party Committee* (established in May 1971)

HSIEH Hsueh-kung	First Secretary	Chairman of Tientsin Municipal Revolutionary Committee; a Party cadre.
WU Tai	Second Secretary	Deputy Political Commissar of Peking Military Region.
LIU Cheng	Secretary	A "responsible person" of PLA units in Tientsin.
WANG Yi	Secretary	A "responsible person" of PLA units in Tientsin.
WANK Man-tien (female)	Secretary	
HSU Cheng	Secretary	
FEI Kuo-chun	Secretary	

Name	Position	Concurrent Posts Held
25. *Yunnan Provincial Party Committee* (established in June 1971)		
CHOU Hsing	First Secretary	Chairman of Yunnan Provincial Revolutionary Committee; Political Commissar of Kunming Military Region.
WANG Pi-cheng	Second Secretary	A military officer.
CHEN Kang	Secretary	Vice-Chairman of Yunnan Provincial Revolutionary Committee; Deputy Commander of Kunming Military Region.
LU Jui-lin	Secretary	Vice-Chairman of Yunnan Provincial Revolutionary Committee; Deputy Commander of Kunming Military Region.
26. *Tibetan Autonomous Regional Party Committee* (established in August 1971)		
JEN Jung	First Secretary	Acting Chairman of Tibetan Autonomous Regional Revolutionary Committee; Political Commissar of Tibet Military Region.
CHEN Ming-yi	Secretary	Vice-Chairman of Tibetan Autonomous Regional Revolutionary Committee; Deputy Commander of Tibet Military Region.
T'IEN Pao	Secretary	Vice-Chairman of Tibetan Autonomous Regional Revolutionary Committee; military officer.

YANG Tung-sheng	Secretary
FENG Ko-ta	Secretary
KAO Sheng-hsuan	Secretary
PA Sang (female)	Secretary

27. *Szechwan Provincial Party Committee* (established in August 1971)

CHANG Kuo-hua	First Secretary	Chairman of Szechwan Provincial Revolutionary Committee; First Political Commissar of Chengtu Military Region.
LIANG Hsing-chu	Second Secretary	Vice-Chairman of Szechwan Provincial Revolutionary Committee; Commander of Chengtu Military Region.
LI Ta-chang	Secretary	
HSIEH Chia-hsiang	Secretary	Deputy Political Commissar of Chengtu Military Region.
TUAN Chun-i	Secretary	
HSIEH Cheng-jung	Secretary	
HSU Chih	Secretary	
HO Yun-feng	Secretary	

28. *Ningsia Hui Autonomous Regional Party Committee* (established in August 1971)

KANG Chien-min	First Secretary	Chairman of Ningsia Hui Autonomous Regional Revolutionary Committee; Political Commissar of Lanchow Military Region.

Name	Position	Concurrent Posts Held
KAO Jui	Second Secretary	
CHANG Kuei-chin	Secretary	
WANG Chih-chiang	Deputy Secretary	Vice-Chairman of Ningsia Hui Autonomous Regional Revolutionary Committee; an administrative cadre.
SHAO Ching-wa	Deputy Secretary	
CHAO Chih-chiang (female)	Deputy Secretary	

29. *Heilungkiang Provincial Party Committee* (established in August 1971)

Name	Position	Concurrent Posts Held
WANG Chi-tao	First Secretary	Chairman of Heilungkiang Provincial Revolutionary Committee; Commander of Heilungkiang Military Region.
LIU Kuang-tao	Second Secretary	
FU Kuei-ching	Secretary	
YU Chieh	Secretary	
CHANG Lin-chih	Secretary	

Chen
Chen
10

INDEX